Competency
in English

Competency in English

A LIFE SKILLS APPROACH

Planaria J. Price

Evans Community Adult School

McGraw-Hill Publishing Company

New York St. Louis San Francisco Auckland Bogotá Caracas Hamburg
Lisbon London Madrid Mexico Milan Montreal New Delhi Oklahoma City
Paris San Juan São Paulo Singapore Sydney Tokyo Toronto

To the memory of my father, Harold Price, M.D.,
and to my mother, Janet Price,
this book is dedicated with love.

This is an  book.

Competency in English
A Life Skills Approach

Copyright © 1990 by McGraw-Hill, Inc. All rights reserved.
Printed in the United States of America. Except as
permitted under the United States Copyright act of 1976, no
part of this publication may be reproduced or distributed in
any form or by any means, or stored in a data base or
retrieval system, without the prior written permission
of the publisher.

2   3   4   5   6   7   8   9   0   MAL   MAL   9   5   4   3   2   1   0

ISBN 0-07-556988-4

Library of Congress Cataloging-in-Publication Data

Price, Planaria J.
    Competency in English : a life skills approach / Planaria J.
Price.
    p.   cm.
    ISBN 0-07-556988-4
    1. English language—Textbooks for foreign speakers.   2. Life
skills.   I. Title.
PE1128.P72   1990
428.2'4—dc20

90.5733
CIP

This book was set in Aster by TBH/Typecast, Inc.
The editors were Mary Gill and Joy Gillian.
The project manager was Marian Hartsough.
The production supervisor was Fred Martich.
The text and cover designer was Rick Chafian.
Illustrations were done by Valerie Winemiller.
Malloy Lithographing was printer and binder.

Realia credits:
page 15, Reprinted with permission © Carlton Cards; *page 104,*
Reprinted with permission by Wells Fargo Bank; *page 140,* Courtesy of
Campbell Soup Company; *pages 141 and 142,* Reprinted by permission
of General Mills, Inc.; *page 174,* Reprinted with permission of Scantron
Corporation.

Acknowledgments

I would like to give a very large thank you to Mary McVey Gill, editor par excellence, for her patience with my stubbornness; to Marian Hartsough, for her excellent production work; to Laurie Blass, who helped refine and streamline the writing; to Pam Hartmann, for her warmth and encouragement; to my delightful and loving students at Evans Community Adult School, who, for the past seventeen years, have helped create this book with their questions, their needs, and their stories; and, most of all, a thank you with deep love to Euphronia and to Murray, who let me take all that time away from them so that I could finally finish this book.

Thanks to the following reviewers for their comments, both favorable and critical, which contributed to the development of this project:

Karen Batt
Erik Beukenkamp
Phillip Borchers
Martin Conroy
Joy Durighello
Charles Elerick
Lois Feldman
Frances Finch
Dean Jensen

Gail Kellersberger
Elaine Kirn
Charles Parish
Betsy Soden
Paula Sunderman
Kent Sutherland
Elizabeth Templin
Deborah Weaver
Bernice M. Weiss

Contents

Preface

RATIONALE

Competency in English: A Life Skills Approach was designed to answer the questions your students have as it teaches them a practical, everyday English they can use in their daily lives. It was written for intermediate students with a basic background in English grammar and vocabulary. The lessons were developed, written, taught, rewritten, taught, etc., over a period of seventeen years and used by a very large number of students. The material was designed to incorporate the questions, needs (both linguistic and social), and experiences of the students into a book that will stimulate them to learn English and teach them various life skills along with language.

ORGANIZATION OF THE TEXT

Considering the time frames of most ESL classes, the diversity of the students, and the differences in students' abilities and needs, we chose to divide the book into ten chapters. The topics are the most crucial subjects that the students need to learn about in order to function in an English-speaking community: for example, how to meet people; basic information on social interaction; how to use a bank, the post office, etc.; and how to get a job. Learning about culture while learning a language is a stimulating experience for students, and all the concepts and vocabulary taught will be constantly reinforced when they go out into the "real world."

Each chapter has an opener and four parts. The opener consists of two pages with pictures to introduce the theme and key vocabulary. These pages lend themselves to informal, nonthreatening class discussions, in which the teacher can elicit comments from the students while presenting vocabulary. Section 1 contains two passages in which the new vocabulary appears in a cultural context relevant to the adult foreign student. The passages can be used for listening comprehension and/or for reading. The short paragraphs also lend themselves to quick dictations. After each passage is read (silently by the students or aloud by the teacher or by the class), there are several true/false questions to test the students' comprehension and generate some discussion. Then a vocabulary reinforcement exercise follows, providing additional contexts/examples of the vocabulary items. Section 1 ends with discussion questions that can be done as a class, in groups, in pairs, or even assigned for written work.

Section 2 of each chapter reinforces the vocabulary and theme of Section 1 and offers an inductive approach to teaching the cultural differences between the US/Canada and the students' native cultures. Most of the material in this section is taken from real-life experiences of real students and should be of practical concern to other nonnative speakers. Again, these situations can be discussed with the whole class, in groups, or in pairs. If the students are confident enough of their English, they can even organize panel discussions or debates to be presented to the whole class.

Section 3 presents conversation practice using real-life expressions that the students can use and will hear in their daily experiences. There are many role-playing activities. Again, these can be done as a class, in groups, or in pairs.

Section 4 contains realia and a writing component, usually emphasizing practical tasks such as filling out forms or applications, writing checks, etc. It also contains cartoons, short articles, and other features, depending on the topic of the chapter. The chapter then ends with open-ended activities. These encourage the students to pursue the topic on their own outside class and then share their findings with the others. Here, again, the idea is reinforced that learning English is the same as living English: it must be practiced in the real world in real situations. When appropriate, names and addresses of community resources are provided along with these activities.

Throughout the book, crucial grammar concepts appear, integrated with other materials rather than taught in isolation. For example, the use of the tag ending is prominent in Chapter 1; *must* and *might* are reviewed in Chapter 2, and structures such as the present perfect, conditional, comparatives, and the use of *very* vs. *too* are reviewed throughout the book. If a teacher has a class that is weak in grammar background, supplemental grammar exercises could be used, but we find informal grammar presentation and actual use of the structures in context to be the most effective way of teaching grammar at this level.

I have tried to make this a conversational book that is easy and fun to teach and hope that both teachers and students enjoy learning from it as much as my students and I enjoyed creating it.

P.J.P.

Competency
in English

CHAPTER 1

Meeting People

Look at these pictures. Think (in English)
about what you see. Study the words
and talk about the scenes.

This picture shows:
1. strangers introducing themselves
2. people shaking hands

These people are:
3. breaking the ice by making small talk
4. enjoying a casual potlock picnic
5. finding something in common

These people are:
6. at a formal gathering
7. being curious
8. having hors d'oeuvres

These are:
9. invitations, sent in advance
10. gifts to bring the host or hostess
11. letters that mean "Please tell me if you can come to the party."

Getting Together

PART A: MAKING NEW FRIENDS

Read this passage to yourself quickly. Don't worry if you don't know all of the words. Just try to understand them in context (by reading the words around them).

Most Americans and Canadians are friendly and curious, interested in meeting new people and learning about their lives. Since many Americans move frequently, they have to leave old friends or family and make new friends. For these and other reasons, formal introductions are usually not necessary, and it is acceptable to introduce yourself to people at parties, on your job, or even on the bus or at the supermarket. On the other hand, you must be very careful with strangers.

At a party, or in any social situation, introduce yourself when you meet someone for the first time by saying your name clearly and slowly. Then shake hands or simply smile at the person you are meeting. After the introduction, make a little "small talk" to break the ice—talk about something simple so that you can both relax: the weather, sports, the hors d'oeuvres you're eating, etc. Then Americans usually ask one another about their work or school. The answers tell them if they have anything in common. You can ask strangers polite questions about their jobs, their families, politics, etc. It is considered impolite, however, to ask North Americans* personal questions about their age, religion, salary, or their weight. In the cultures of the United States and Canada, you can talk freely to strangers about personal things that they can control, but most North Americans prefer not to talk to strangers about those things they cannot change, such as their age, salary, or religion.

---

*In this book, the term *North American* will refer to people from Canada and the United States. Technically, it should also include people from Mexico, but since Mexicans often refer to Americans as *norteamericanos* and since *North American* is much shorter than "people from the United States and Canada," we will use it here, with apologies to our Mexican friends.

Most important of all, relax. Making new friends can be fun. You may find, by coincidence, that you know some of the same people, have had similar experiences, or have common interests with someone you meet for the first time. It's a small world, after all, and friendly get-togethers can make it even smaller.

True or False?

Answer *true* or *false*; then correct the false statements. Read aloud the sentences in the passage that led you to your answers.

1. Most North Americans are not interested in making new friends.

2. You should never introduce yourself to a stranger.

3. North Americans usually make small talk at parties by discussing simple, polite topics.

4. "Are you a Christian?" would be a polite question to ask someone at a party in the United States or Canada.

Vocabulary

Guess the meanings of the underlined words from the contexts. Then match them with the definitions that follow. Write the letters of the definitions in the parentheses (___).

1. Making new friends is not easy; you should be friendly and <u>curious</u> (___) and ask many questions.

2. Strangers often find, by <u>coincidence</u> (___), that they share similar experiences or that they <u>have</u> friends <u>in common</u> (___).

3. It's not easy meeting people for the first time. After you introduce yourself, try to <u>make small talk</u> (___) to <u>break the ice</u> (___). If you talk about simple things such as the weather, the food you're eating, or a television program, it will help you relax.

4. It's easier to break the ice when eating, so at most parties people serve <u>hors d'oeuvres</u> (___) (pronounced /or dervs/), such as cheese and crackers, potato chips and dip, and little meatballs, before dinner.

Definitions

a. talk about things of little importance

b. a combination of chance events that seem planned, but weren't

c. wanting to know and learn

d. snacks before a meal

e. have the same (ideas, experiences, and so on)

f. make people feel relaxed and friendly

PART B: FORMAL AND INFORMAL GET-TOGETHERS

Read this passage to yourself quickly. Try to understand new words in context.

Because so many Americans and Canadians want to make new friends, they have many kinds of get-togethers or social gatherings. These include formal parties, parties for special purposes or occasions, and informal parties where friends may meet just to chat or because they haven't seen one another for a long time.

One informal or casual kind of social gathering is a potluck party. At a potluck, each guest brings some food. To prevent unfortunate coincidences, the host or hostess sometimes suggests the kinds of food each guest should bring (hors d'oeuvres, salads, main courses, desserts, etc.). They don't want a party with 20 different pies or cakes and nothing else!

Another kind of get-together is an "open house" where the host or hostess invites a lot of people and serves hors d'oeuvres. The guests find many strangers at these parties, and the host or hostess will try to introduce people who might have something in common. If the host or hostess is too busy, the guests introduce themselves to one another. Since the purpose of the party is to meet new people and talk, there is usually no music or dancing.

For a formal party, people often send written invitations weeks in advance; these usually include an R.S.V.P., which means, "Please respond"—tell the host or hostess whether or not you are going to attend. People usually invite friends to an informal party by telephone. In either situation, it's nice to bring a small gift (such as some flowers or a box of candy) for the host or hostess.

True or False?

Answer *true* or *false*; then correct the false statements. Read aloud the sentences in the passage that led you to your answers.

1. A potluck party is a formal gathering at a restaurant.

2. At an open house, most of the guests know each other.

3. There is a lot of music and dancing at an open house.

4. It's a good idea to take a small gift to a party.

Vocabulary

Guess the meanings of the underlined words from the contexts. Then match them with the definitions that follow. Write the letters of the definitions in the parentheses (___).

1. A potluck (___) party is common on the Fourth of July. Someone always brings potato salad, and others bring hot dogs and watermelon.

2. Potlucks are usually casual (___) parties; men don't wear ties and women don't wear formal dresses.

3. For <u>formal</u> (___) parties, people usually receive <u>invitations</u> (___) a few weeks <u>in advance</u> (___).

4. Always be sure to reply to the <u>R.S.V.P.</u> (___) so that the <u>host or hostess</u> (___) will know if you are coming.

5. People often have <u>get-togethers</u> (___) on weekends between 4:00 P.M. and 7:00 P.M. or from 8:00 P.M. to 11:00 P.M.

Definitions

a. not casual

b. not formal, relaxed

c. request to answer "yes" or "no" to an invitation

d. the person who gives a party or dinner

e. before

f. a request for someone to come to an event

g. social gatherings

h. parties where the guests bring the food

Discussion Questions

Discuss these questions with your classmates.

1. It is acceptable to talk to strangers in some situations, but should you go to their houses or give them your address? Why or why not?

2. Where is it acceptable to talk to strangers in the United States or Canada? In your culture?

3. How do people introduce themselves and greet each other in the United States and Canada? In your culture? (Examples: by shaking hands, bowing, etc.)

4. In making small talk, what questions are common in the United States or Canada? In your culture? What questions are impolite?

5. If you were invited to a potluck party, what food would you want to bring? Do you have potlucks in your culture? Explain.

Polite Behavior in Formal Situations

SITUATIONS

Discuss these situations with your classmates. Choose the best answer, in your opinion. Then compare your answers with the cultural notes that follow.

1. In the United States or Canada, when someone invites you to a dinner party for a specific time, you should:
   a. be late
   b. come a half-hour early
   c. arrive just on time

2. In the United States or Canada, when someone invites you to his or her home for a party or for dinner, you should:
   a. not bring anything except an empty stomach
   b. bring hors d'oeuvres, fruit, or a cake
   c. bring a small gift such as flowers, something to drink, or candy

3. In the United States or Canada, when you introduce a person to someone else, the order of the person's name is:
   a. first name, then last name (surname)
   b. last name, first name, then middle name
   c. first name, middle name, then maiden name

4. When meeting people for the first time in the United States or Canada, you should:
   a. hug and kiss them
   b. shake hands with them
   c. bow, but not touch them

CULTURAL NOTES

1a. It's impolite to arrive at a dinner party more than 15 to 20 minutes late. Although there will probably be hors d'oeuvres before dinner, the host or hostess usually waits for all of the guests before serving the food. If someone is late, the food may be spoiled, and so might the host or hostess's mood. If you find you will have to be late, call and tell them to start without you.

1b. It's even worse to be early! The host or hostess will probably not be ready. (They wouldn't want you to find them sweeping the dust under the carpet!) If you are early, drive or walk around the block a few times, or just sit in your car until the right time.

1c. It's often important to arrive at a party on time. Some get-togethers, especially formal dinner parties and surprise parties, depend on exact arrival times. On the other hand, for open houses, the host or hostess invites the guests to arrive and leave between specific times, so you can arrive at any time within the times he or she gives you.

2a. Yes, it's nice to bring an empty stomach, but it's even nicer to bring a small gift.

2b. Unless the party is a potluck, it's best not to bring any food because the host or hostess would then have to serve it. He or she has planned the dinner or snacks, and the food you bring might not fit the menu. On the other hand, if the host or hostess is a close friend of yours, he or she might ask you to bring some food.

2c. It's nice to bring a simple gift to a party. The gift should not cost a lot, or you might embarrass the host or hostess. Flowers (but not a dozen long-stemmed red roses!), a box of candy, a bottle of inexpensive (but good) wine, some pretty soap for the guest bathroom, and similar gifts are appropriate. Never bring money as a gift.

3a. In an introduction, the customary order of a name is: (1) the given name (the name your friends and family call you), (2) the family name or surname. In other words, the first name comes *first*. It's important not only to learn and remember names, but to repeat them often in conversation. After the introduction, we usually call friends and acquaintances by their first names. Employers or older people may want you to call them by their titles and last names, such as "Mr. Jones," "Mrs. Smith," "Ms. Johnson," or "Dr. Brown."

3b. North Americans don't normally give their last names first, or only their last names, in conversation. Use last names first, with commas after them, only in alphabetical lists or on written forms (for example: Smith, Jack). North Americans often use middle names on forms, but not usually in conversation.

3c. A maiden name is a woman's last name at birth. In the United States and Canada, after a woman marries, she normally takes the last name of her husband in place of her maiden name. Banks and other agencies often ask for a mother's maiden name as proof of identity. It is now becoming common, however, for women to keep their maiden names after marriage. Some add the names of their husbands to their maiden names with a hyphen. (For example, Mary Smith marries Tom Jones, and she becomes Mary Smith-Jones instead of Mary Jones.)

4a. North Americans might kiss a close friend on the cheek in greeting (but never on the lips—unless they are very, very close!). It is not customary for Americans to greet each other with a kiss unless they have not met for a long time.

4b. When you meet people formally, it is customary to shake hands. (This custom comes from ancient times when a stranger opened his right hand to show another person there was no weapon in it.) When you meet someone, it's a good idea to repeat the person's name so you can remember it. If you don't understand the name, ask for it again and spell it. (It's embarrassing to forget someone's name when you are becoming friends.) Then shake hands firmly, right hand to right hand. Don't shake hands like a dead fish, but don't break the other person's fingers either. And don't hold on too long, or the person may become uncomfortable. Be sure to smile and look the person in the eyes. When friends meet informally, they usually greet one another without shaking hands.

4c. No; people don't bow in the United States or Canada.

Informal Get-Togethers

EXTENDING INVITATIONS

Instead of sending a written invitation, most people call their friends on the telephone to tell them about an informal party a few days or weeks in advance.

Practice this conversation in pairs:

CHRIS: Hello.

ROSA: Hi, Chris. This is Rosa. I'm having

a potluck dinner	two weeks from Sunday.
a dinner party	on June 21st.
an open house	on Valentine's Day.

	interesting people.
I hope you can come. I invited some	really nice guys.
	really sweet girls.

I know you'll enjoy meeting them.

| CHRIS: | I'd love to come, Rosa. | | |
| | Thanks for inviting me, Rosa. | Can I bring anything? |

| ROSA: | Could you bring some hors d'oeuvres? |
| | Nothing, thank you. |

CHRIS: What should I wear?

| ROSA: It's | casual. |
| | informal. |

CHRIS: O.K. Rosa. Thanks for inviting me. See you there.
Bye.

ROSA: Bye-bye.

Role-play

Invite a classmate to an imaginary party. After your partner says "yes," let him or her invite you, using different expressions. (Your partner could also say, "I'm sorry. I can't make it, but thank you for inviting me anyway.")

INTRODUCING YOURSELF

How do you start a conversation with a stranger? One easy way is to ask a question.

Practice this conversation in pairs:

REIKO: Excuse me, but have you seen Rosa?
CHRIS: Yes, she was just here. Why?
REIKO: Oh, I wanted to talk to her. By the way, my name is Reiko Yamamoto.
CHRIS: Hi! Excuse me. I didn't catch your name.
REIKO: (*speaking clearly and slowly*) Reiko Yamamoto.
CHRIS: Hi, Lako.
REIKO: No, it's Reiko.
CHRIS: Oh, hello, Dako.
REIKO: No, Reiko!
CHRIS: Excuse me, could you please spell your name?
REIKO: Of course. It's R-E-I-K-O.
CHRIS: Ahhh. *Reiko.* Is Reiko your first name?
REIKO: Yes. Yamamoto is my last name.
CHRIS: Well, Reiko. I'm very pleased to meet you. My name is Jean-Christophe Prémel, but my friends call me Chris for short.
REIKO: (*They shake hands while smiling and looking each other in the eyes.*) I'm happy to meet you, Chris.

Role-play

Walk around the room and introduce yourself to your classmates. Be sure to shake hands, look each other in the eyes, and pronounce names correctly. If you can't understand a name, ask the person to spell it for you.

STARTING A CONVERSATION

After you are introduced, or introduce yourself to someone, you will want to break the ice by starting a conversation. Use small talk to find out what you have in common.

Practice this conversation in pairs:

ROSA: José Antonio Ramos, I'd like you to meet my friend, Anh Thi Nguyen. Anh, this is José. I think you two might have a lot in common.
JOSÉ: I'm glad to meet you, Anh.
ANNIE: I'm pleased to meet you too, José. Please call me Annie.
JOSÉ: This is a nice party, isn't it, Annie?
ANNIE: Yes, it is—and such lovely weather.
JOSÉ: Have you known Rosa long?
ANNIE: No. We met two months ago, but we're good friends.
JOSÉ: Where are you from?
ANNIE: Well, I was born in Vietnam, but I grew up in Paris.

JOSÉ: Really? I was born in Venezuela, but we moved to Paris when I
       was ten.
ANNIE: What a small world! José, what do you do?
JOSÉ: I'm an artist. And you?
ANNIE: What a coincidence! I taught art in Paris.
JOSÉ: How interesting. Did you come here to San Francisco with your
       husband?
ANNIE: Oh no. I'm single. Ummmmmm, are you here with your wife?
JOSÉ: (*smiling*) No, I'm not married either. Say, Annie, what did you
       bring to the party?
ANNIE: I brought different kinds of dips. And you?
JOSÉ: I can't believe the coincidences, Annie. I brought different kinds
       of chips. Let's go over to the hors d'oeuvre table and try them
       out.
ANNIE: I'd love to. I'm glad we have so much in common.

Role-play

Have an imaginary party in your class. Choose several hosts or hostesses; everyone else will be the guests. Walk around the room meeting
people. (Don't sit at your desks! There usually aren't many chairs at a
party.) Use some small talk to break the ice—and be sure that it's in
English!

EXPRESSING THANKS INFORMALLY

After a get-together you may want to call and thank the host or hostess the next day. Be sure you don't call too early in the morning. Your
friend will probably be tired from all the work of the party.
    Practice this conversation in pairs:

ROSA: Hello.
ANNIE: Hi Rosa, this is Annie. I just wanted to thank you again for
       inviting me to your wonderful party yesterday. I had a great
       time.
ROSA: Thank you for coming, Annie. I'm so glad you enjoyed yourself.
       Ummmmm, are you going to see José again?
ANNIE: Oh, yes. As a matter of fact, we're meeting for dinner in an
       hour.
ROSA: Annie, that's fantastic! Well, have a good time and call me as
       soon as you can to tell me all about it.
ANNIE: O.K., Rosa. I feel so nervous I've got butterflies in my stomach*!
ROSA: Good luck, Annie. Bye-bye.
ANNIE: Bye-bye.

---

*to have butterflies in your stomach** = *to feel nervous*

Role-play

Role-play the following with your classmates:

1. José calls Rosa and thanks her for the party.
2. Reiko calls Rosa and thanks her for the party.
3. Annie calls Rosa after Annie and José have dinner.

SECTION 4
Bits and Pieces

FORMAL WRITTEN INVITATIONS

For a formal party or get-together for an occasion such as a birthday, a wedding, a baby shower, or an anniversary, people usually mail invitations two or three weeks in advance.

Read this invitation and answer the questions.

It's a very special date . . .
Please come and help us celebrate!

Occasion *Grigor's Citizenship*

Date *Saturday, September 11*

Time *6:30 p.m. (dinner)*

Place *717 N. Figueroa #231*
(dressy)

R.S.V.P.   555-7151

1. What will the party celebrate?
2. What day of the week is it?
3. What kind of clothes should the guests wear?
4. Why will the guests call 555-7151?
5. What time should the guests arrive?

Now read this envelope and answer the questions.

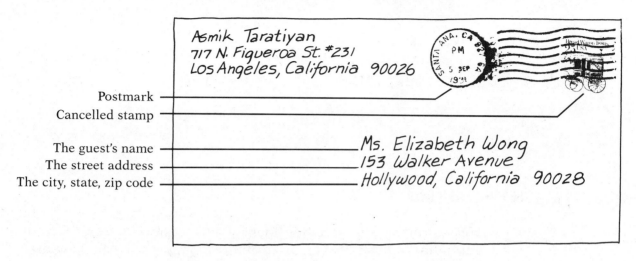

1. Who is the hostess?
2. Who is the guest?
3. Where does the guest live?
4. What is the guest's zip code?
5. What is the street address of the hostess?
6. Has the letter been mailed?

FORMAL THANK-YOU NOTES

After a party, you might want to send a short thank-you note. In the note, you thank the host or hostess for inviting you, tell what was nice about the party, and then close by expressing thanks again.

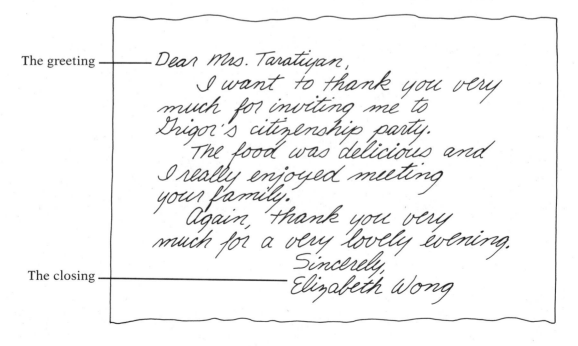

WRITING AN INVITATION AND THANK-YOU NOTE

Following the directions below, design an invitation to an imaginary party; then exchange invitations with a classmate. Read the invitation, imagine the get-together, and then write an appropriate thank-you note. Be sure to address the envelope and draw a stamp at the top.

To make the invitation, fold a piece of paper into four equal parts. On the front, draw a picture or write in big letters. Inside, write the information—the occasion, the date, the place, etc.

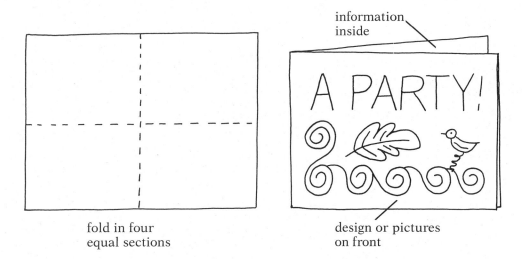

fold in four
equal sections

information
inside

design or pictures
on front

With another piece of paper, make an "envelope" by folding the paper *almost* in half, leaving one-half inch at the top. Put the invitation inside and fold over the one-half inch. Address the envelope to a classmate and draw a stamp at the top.

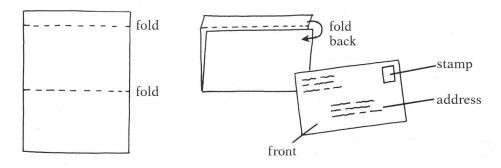

fold

fold

fold
back

stamp

address

front

HUMOR

The following cartoons make fun of the custom of small talk in the United States and Canada. Read and discuss them with your classmates.

ADVICE FROM ZENOBIA

In newspaper advice columns, readers write to the columnist and ask what to do about personal problems. Read the letter to Zenobia. Talk with your classmates about the possible solutions to the problem. Then read the advice columnist's answer. Discuss whether you agree with the advice or not.

Dear Zenobia

TALK ABOUT WEATHER WILL BREAK THE ICE

By Zenobia Neal

Dear Zenobia,

There's this real cute guy who takes the same bus I take every day on my way to work. I just know we have a lot in common and could really get to be good friends. I keep waiting for him to say something to me, but he doesn't. Please tell me how to start a conversation with him.

E.K. from S.F.

Dear E.K.,

So that both of you can relax, start with some small talk. Smile pleasantly and say, "Good morning. Isn't it cold (or warm, or lovely, or windy) out?"

If he has any interest in you, he'll continue the conversation. If he doesn't, at least you tried.

OPEN-ENDED ACTIVITIES

Choose one or more of the following activities to do outside of class. When you finish, tell the class what you've learned.

1. Write a letter to your local newspaper's advice columnist asking a question about meeting people. See what kind of answer you get — it might even appear in the newspaper.

2. Read the cartoons in your local newspaper for one week and see how many of them discuss how people meet each other and what they say and do.

3. If you're fortunate enough to be invited to an American party, go and then share your experiences with your classmates. If you don't know any Americans, have your own party and invite your classmates, but try to make it a typical "American" party with little or no dancing or music and a lot of talking — in English!

4. Watch situation comedy programs on television and pay close attention to how the Americans talk to each other. Do they shake hands? What kind of small talk do they make? What do they do at their parties? What are they wearing?

CHAPTER **2**

Common Courtesy
in North America

Look at these pictures. Think (in English)
about what you see. Study the words
and talk about the scenes.

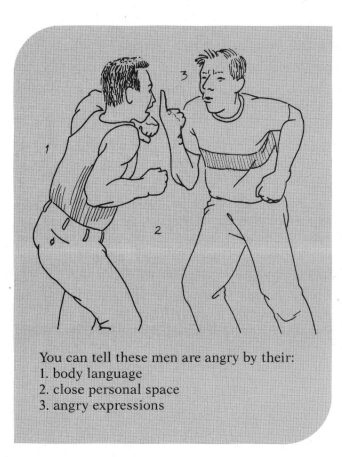

You can tell these men are angry by their:
1. body language
2. close personal space
3. angry expressions

These people are being courteous when they:
4. yawn
5. cough
6. burp

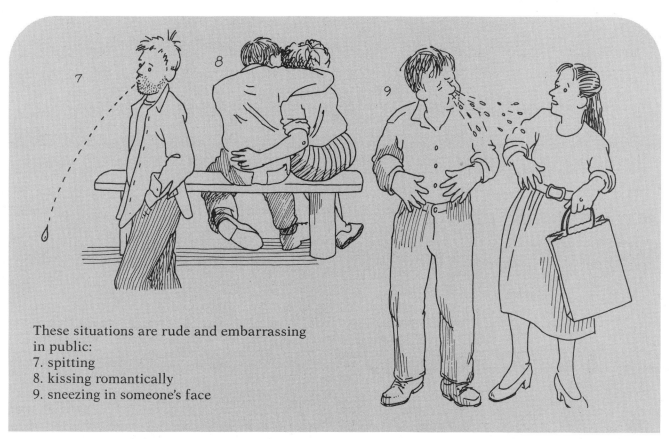

These situations are rude and embarrassing
in public:
7. spitting
8. kissing romantically
9. sneezing in someone's face

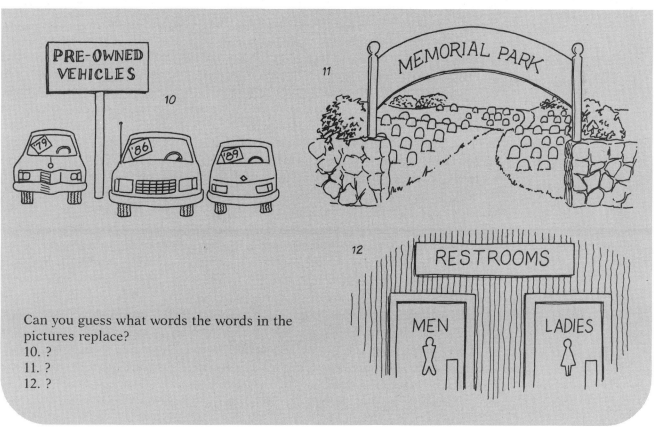

Can you guess what words the words in the
pictures replace?
10. ?
11. ?
12. ?

SECTION 1

Spoken and Unspoken Language

PART A: POLITE AND RUDE

Read this passage to yourself quickly. Don't worry if you don't know all of the words. Just try to understand them in context.

You've probably already discovered that learning a foreign language isn't just learning new words and grammar. In order to speak fluently—and to avoid some embarrassing situations—you must learn how to use the words and grammatical structures within the context of the culture.

Not only must you learn the vocabulary, but you must learn which words to choose in which situations. English speakers use a lot of euphemisms—polite, less direct words for things or ideas that may cause embarrassment. Sometimes words with the same meanings produce different feelings in the listeners, so you must choose words carefully depending upon the situation.

Every culture has specific rules of courtesy and certain words for special situations. Different cultures also have customary ways to act and to look at and touch people. What are considered polite manners in one culture might be terribly rude in another. One of the difficulties of learning a foreign language is learning what is considered polite and rude in the culture of that language. The dictionary doesn't tell you this.

Do you remember your first impressions of North Americans (or people from other cultures as well)? Have you noticed that North Americans like to have a lot of personal space around them and feel very uncomfortable if they have to stand too close to others? Perhaps you wondered why they stood so far away from you.

Were you surprised at the way North Americans eat? Different cultures not only have different foods, but people also eat in different ways. In the United States and Canada, eating is a social occasion, and people like to talk while they eat. North Americans don't make noise or talk while they have food in their mouths. One person chews while a second person talks, and then the second person talks while the first person chews! Learning to do this is almost like learning a new dance step. Many foreigners are surprised at this and at how many different foods Americans eat with their fingers: fried chicken, spare ribs, pizza, french fries, sandwiches, corn on the cob, fruit, etc.

True or False?

Answer *true* or *false*; then correct the false statements. Read aloud the sentences in the passage that led you to your answers.

1. Euphemisms are polite or less direct ways of saying things people are uncomfortable about.

2. Understanding a language also means understanding the culture.

3. North Americans like to stand close to each other.

4. North Americans don't talk until after they have finished a meal.

Vocabulary

Guess the meanings of the underlined words from the contexts. Then match them with the definitions that follow. Write the letters of the definitions in the parentheses (___).

1. It usually takes five years of study to speak a language <u>fluently</u> (___). In fact, it took you about five years just to learn the grammar and vocabulary of your own language, didn't it?

2. In most countries, it is common <u>courtesy</u> (___) not to <u>chew</u> (___) with your mouth open and it is <u>rude</u> (___) to make noise, especially when eating soup!

3. In the United States and Canada, it is <u>customary</u> (___) not to stand too close to strangers.

4. North Americans dislike crowds because they feel uncomfortable when other people invade their <u>personal space</u> (___).

5. Politicians often use <u>euphemisms</u> (___) to avoid <u>embarrassment</u> (___) or stating an unpleasant truth directly.

Definitions

a. with ease and comfort

b. polite, less direct ways of saying things that people aren't comfortable about

c. not polite

d. the distance people need around them in order to feel comfortable

e. feeling uncomfortable or ashamed

f. done most of the time; usual

g. good manners; politeness

h. to crush food with the teeth

PART B: BODY LANGUAGE

Read this passage to yourself quickly. Try to understand new words in context.

We call actions that communicate ideas without the use of words *gestures* or *body language*. Just as each culture has a different spoken language, so each culture has different body language. Think about the body language you've seen since you've been here—some of these gestures may have opposite meanings in your culture. Learning about these actions is a necessary part of learning American English—and a lot of fun, too.

People use their hands differently in each culture. In the United States and Canada, people often shake hands when they greet others. They may pat someone on the back as a sign of friendliness. They even use the idiom "a pat on the back" to mean a sign of encouragement. In some countries, however, people feel that such actions are rude. In some countries it is polite to cover your mouth when you talk or laugh. North Americans cover their mouths only when they yawn, cough, sneeze, or burp. What about using your hands to get someone's attention? In some countries people clap their hands, snap their fingers, or point. In the United States and Canada, however, people just try to "catch a person's eye" (get the person's attention by looking into his or her eyes).

Kissing and hugging in public places can cause people great discomfort or great happiness depending on their culture. In North America, it's O.K. to hug or kiss in public, especially at airports, but the action shouldn't last too long!

What you do with your eyes is also different in each culture. In some countries it's a sign of respect not to look directly at someone such as a police officer, a teacher, a mother-in-law, etc. In North America, if you don't look directly at people, they might not trust you. In some countries it's O.K. for men to stare directly at women. However, this makes most American women very uncomfortable. Learning the body language of Americans can be fun, and once you learn it you'll be speaking English like a native.

True or False?

Answer *true* or *false*; then correct the false statements. Read aloud the sentences in the passage that led you to your answers.

1. Body language is learning the parts of the body.

2. It's acceptable to stare at a pretty woman in the United States or Canada.

3. Americans cover their mouths when they cough, yawn, and sneeze.

4. In North America, it is acceptable to snap your fingers to get someone's attention.

Vocabulary

Divide into groups of four. Working together, try to match the body language in the pictures with the words. (Hint: Say the sound and see how the sound imitates the action.)

1. ___ yawn
2. ___ clap
3. ___ snap one's finger
4. ___ hug
5. ___ spit
6. ___ snore
7. ___ whistle
8. ___ whisper

Discussion Questions

Discuss these questions with your classmates.

1. Do Americans and Canadians do anything that surprises or shocks you? Describe these actions.

2. Do people in your culture prefer more or less personal space than North Americans do? Do they look directly at each other when they talk?

3. Do people hug and kiss on the streets of your country? How do you feel about this?

4. Are the actions and noises in the vocabulary exercise above polite, acceptable, or rude in North America? In your culture? Explain.

SECTION 2

Polite, Acceptable, or Rude?

SITUATIONS

Discuss these situations with your classmates. Choose the best answer, in your opinion. Then compare your answers with the cultural notes that follow.

1. The police in a North American city stopped Loc Ba Nguyen because his car was similar to one just used in a bank robbery. He was frightened. To show his respect, he did not look directly at the officers. What probably happened?
   a. Since his car was not the same one used in the bank robbery, the police released him immediately.
   b. The police took him to jail until they found the real robbers.
   c. The police kept him by the side of the road while they phoned for a computer check on his identity and the car registration.

2. At the movies, a man had a very bad cold. He was sniffling because his nose was running. After he blew his nose with his fingers, he wiped them on his pants and then spit on the floor. The people sitting near him were shocked because:
   a. it's rude to be in public with a bad cold
   b. it's rude to blow your nose in public
   c. it's rude to spit in public

3. Janet was in a bad mood at the office. The secretary at the next desk kept covering her mouth and coughing, and Janet's boss— standing rather close to her—had forgotten his deodorant and had eaten a garlic and onion omelet for breakfast. Janet's stomach was growling and she thought the 12:00 lunch break would never come. She was probably in a bad mood because:
   a. her boss was standing too close to her, and the air was unpleasant-smelling
   b. the secretary was coughing
   c. both a and b

4. Irene and Bill Clark invited Hitomi Tetsuya to dinner. The Clarks served, among other things, fried chicken and corn on the cob. In addition, there was a little bowl of water with a lemon beside each plate. What probably happened?

   a. Hitomi felt insulted because they served corn on the cob at dinner.

   b. She drank the bowl of water with the lemon.

   c. She ate the chicken and corn with her fingers and then washed her fingers in the water.

5. Jeanie Cohen was very pretty. As she walked down a Chicago street, a man at the corner stared at her—from her toes to her head and down again. Then he said, "Pretty lady," and whistled. Another man drove by honking his horn at her. Jeanie felt uncomfortable because:

   a. she didn't think the men were handsome enough

   b. she felt afraid, and the loud horn annoyed her

   c. both a and b

CULTURAL NOTES

1a. If Loc had looked directly at the officers, smiled, and said, "What seems to be the trouble, officers?" they probably would have looked at his driver's license and car registration, told him he could go, and apologized for stopping him.

1b. An important American law states that people are innocent until a court of law proves them guilty. Since the car was obviously not the one used in the robbery, there was no reason that Loc would have to go to jail.

1c. The police may have done a computer check on him because of Loc's body language. By not looking directly at the officers, Loc made the American officers think that he was hiding something. Clearly Loc wasn't the bank robber, but the officer checked on Loc's record because he was acting suspiciously.

2a. The best place to be when you're sick is home. Unfortunately, some people go out in public and to work when they're ill and they spread their germs. It's not polite, but it's very common.

2b. It's unpleasant to sit next to someone who's sniffling, but sometimes—especially if the person has allergies—his or her nose keeps running. It's O.K. to blow your nose in public as long as you use a handkerchief or tissue, but be sure to put it away after using it. It's more polite to blow your nose quietly than to sniffle or keep leaving the room.

2c. A hundred years ago men chewed tobacco, and spitting was an accepted custom. Now, spitting in sinks, trash cans, or on the ground is considered very rude and unsanitary. If you have a special problem and need to spit, spit quietly into a tissue and throw it away in the trash.

3a. Standing too close to people (invading their personal space) is rude in the United States and Canada. Most North Americans prefer to stand about two or three feet away from each other when conversing in public places. Janet's boss annoyed her because he was invading her personal space and he smelled bad. You've probably noticed from television and radio commercials that North Americans like to be very clean. They consider it impolite to have body odors or bad breath, or to wear too much perfume or aftershave. They take a lot of showers, brush their teeth often, and use breath-fresheners and deodorants.

3b.   While it can be annoying to hear coughing, hiccuping, or sneezing, these actions are not considered rude in North America, as long as people keep their mouths covered and turn away from others. A growling stomach is also acceptable because it is uncontrollable.

3c.   The best answer is a.

4a.   Hitomi might have been insulted because in many countries corn on the cob is food for farm animals only, while in other countries it is an informal snack and never served to dinner guests. In the United States, eating corn on the cob at meals is a summertime treat. Americans even have special plates and cob-holders for this dish. They put butter, salt, and pepper on the corn; put the little holders in each end of the cob; then pick it up in both hands and eat it. Try it. You'll like it.

4b.   In some countries, especially Japan, there is a very delicious, clear soup that looks just like the water in the "finger bowls" that people use in the United States and Canada. But the water in finger bowls is for washing your fingers after the meal, not for drinking!

4c.   Some foods that Americans eat with their fingers are: fried chicken, spare ribs, pizza, and corn on the cob. When in doubt, do what other people are doing. When you're finished, dip your fingers in the finger bowl to clean them.

5a.   It is impolite in the United States to stare openly at people. Even if the men were handsome, their behavior would have been insulting to an American woman.

5b.   Whistles and noises may be customary in some countries, but in the United States and Canada, these noises make women very uncomfortable. Also, the horn probably bothered her. You should use your horn only in a traffic emergency. In some cities the police will give you a ticket for using your horn at the wrong time. Making noise is really an invasion of someone's privacy, and protection of one's privacy is an American right.

5c.   The best answer is b.

Cultures in Contrast

ASKING FOR INFORMATION

Whenever you aren't sure how to behave in a new situation, don't be afraid to ask! Most people enjoy explaining the habits and customs of their culture.

Practice this conversation in pairs:

IRENE: Hitomi, please take an artichoke.

HITOMI: Thank you, Irene, but I've never had this before. Would you mind showing me how to eat it?

IRENE: Of course! Just watch. Pull off one leaf with your fingers. Dip the leaf in the sauce like this. Then scrape off the fleshy part with your teeth. Don't eat the rest of the leaf—put it in the dish to the side of your plate.

Role-play

Imagine you are having dinner with a classmate from another country. You, the host or hostess, serve your guest a dish from your culture that he or she has never tried. Explain how to eat it. Then change roles.

UNDERSTANDING EUPHEMISMS

As with differences in culture, you might not understand why an American chooses one word in place of another. In pairs, practice this conversation of euphemisms (Conversation 1) and then replace the underlined euphemisms with the "real" words (Conversation 2).

Conversation 1

NATASHA: Are you coming to my party tomorrow?
HELOISE: No, I can't. My aunt just <u>passed away</u> and I have to go to the <u>memorial park</u> for the <u>services</u>.
NATASHA: Oh, Heloise. I'm sorry. How did it happen?
HELOISE: She was a <u>large senior citizen with a little drinking problem</u>. Well, last night she went to the bathroom for a drink of water and drank from the glass that had my uncle's <u>dentures</u>. The shock <u>was too much for her and she expired</u>.

Conversation 2

NATASHA: Are you coming to my party tomorrow?
HELOISE: No, I can't. My aunt just <u>died</u> and I have to go to the <u>cemetery</u> for the <u>funeral</u>.
NATASHA: Oh, Heloise. I'm sorry. How did it happen?
HELOISE: She was <u>fat and old and sometimes drunk</u>. Well, last night she went to the bathroom for a drink of water and drank from the glass that had my uncle's <u>false teeth</u>. The shock <u>killed her</u>.

CONVERSATION ACTIVITY

Using the vocabulary lists below, fill in the blanks twice. First use the euphemisms and then use the "real" words. Discuss how the descriptions differ.

I want you to meet my neighbor. He is _____

and _____. He _____
2   3

and _____. He used to be a _____,
4   5

and now he is a _____ salesman.
6

EUPHEMISMS	"REAL WORDS"
1. slim	skinny
2. not good-looking	ugly
3. is full of interesting information about people	gossips
4. exaggerates a bit	lies
5. sanitation engineer	garbage collector
6. previously owned vehicle	used car

Note: Euphemisms are usually longer and more formal words.

Bits and Pieces

OBSERVING BODY LANGUAGE

Observe the body language of North Americans and fill in the following charts. Then discuss your observations with your classmates, comparing and contrasting American body language with the body language of your culture.

1. Personal space: How close or far do Americans feel comfortable standing with each other? Check (✔) the boxes.

" means inches 12" = one foot	less than 18"	18" to 22"	22" to 28"	28" to 36"	more than 36"
standing in a crowded elevator					
standing in an uncrowded elevator					
talking to strangers					
talking to acquaintances					
talking to friends					

Now put circles (○) in the boxes for the comfortable space in your culture. Discuss the differences.

2. Touching: Watch how Americans kiss each other. Which of the following do they do? Which don't they do? Fill in the chart by answering *Y* for yes, *N* for no, or *S* for sometimes.

	men kiss men	women kiss women	men kiss women	fathers kiss sons	fathers kiss daughters	mothers kiss sons	mothers kiss daughters
on the lips							
on the forehead							
on the cheeks							
on the hand							
in public							

3. Other customs: Which of the following customs are polite in the United States or Canada? Are the same customs polite or rude in your culture? Write *Y* for yes or *N* for no in the appropriate boxes of this chart. Add your own observations at the bottom.

	polite in North America	polite in my country
standing with hands on hips		
standing with arms folded in front of you		
throwing trash in the street (littering)		
standing in the street doing nothing (loitering)		
writing on walls (graffiti)		
spitting on the street		
eating with one hand in your lap and one hand on the table		
putting your fingers in your nose		
cracking your knuckles		
cleaning your teeth with a toothpick		
wearing sunglasses inside		
playing loud music in public		
wearing a hat inside		
teachers sitting on desks		

Now compare and discuss your answers to Observations 1, 2, and 3 with your classmates.

HUMOR

The following cartoons make fun of customs of courtesy in the United States and Canada. Read and discuss them with your classmates.

LIFE IN THE FAST LANE · by BILL BURNS

OPEN-ENDED ACTIVITIES

Choose one or more of the following activities to do outside of class. When you finish, tell the class what you've learned.

1. Read cartoons and news articles and see what more you can learn about body language and euphemisms.

2. Watch situation comedies and drama shows on television and pay special attention to body language. See if you can learn more about what people consider polite and rude in the United States and Canada.

3. Look at advertisements in magazines and watch commercials on television. How many euphemisms can you find?

4. Listen to the traffic reports on the radio and identify the euphemisms.

CHAPTER 3

Emergencies

Look at these pictures. Think (in English) about what you see. Study the words and talk about the scenes.

This is:
1. a robber
2. a victim
3. an emergency

A person whose clothes are on fire should:
4. stop, drop, and roll
5. get immediate first aid

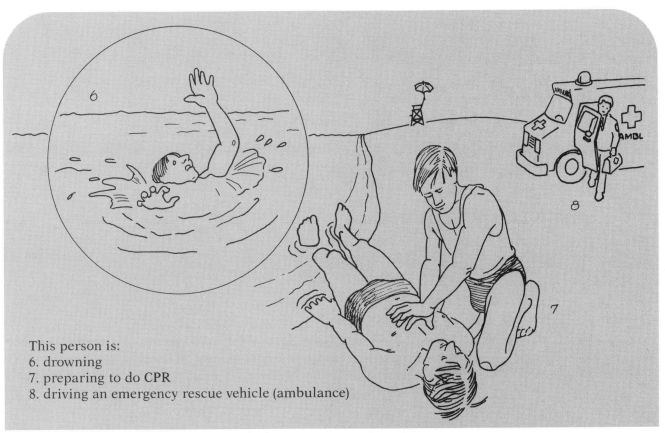

This person is:
6. drowning
7. preparing to do CPR
8. driving an emergency rescue vehicle (ambulance)

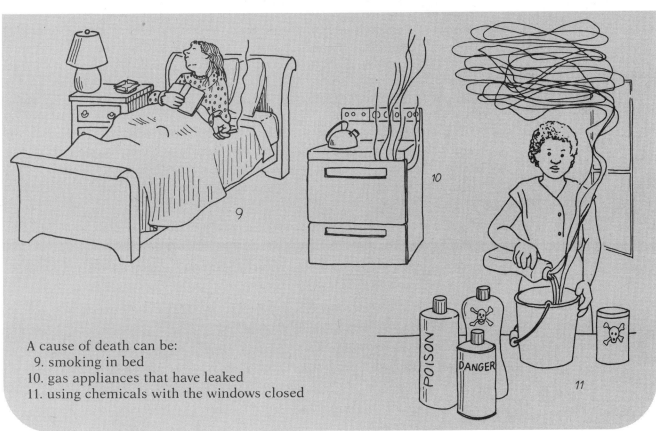

A cause of death can be:
9. smoking in bed
10. gas appliances that have leaked
11. using chemicals with the windows closed

Getting Help

PART A: WHAT TO DO IN AN EMERGENCY

Read this passage to yourself quickly. Don't worry if you don't know all of the words. Just try to understand them in context.

In the United States and Canada, the police, fire, and paramedic departments are free public services to anyone in need, especially in an emergency. Don't be afraid to ask for help. Because emergencies are unplanned, you must be prepared for them and know what to do immediately. It's best to plan for an emergency in advance, so if it does happen you can react quickly and automatically. In an emergency, acting quickly can make the difference between life and death.

Be sure to paste the direct numbers of your police, fire, and paramedic services on your phone. In most cities of the United States, the number *911* will connect you quickly with several emergency services. If you can't remember the number, you can always dial *0* for operator, but it will take more time. When you call for help, speak clearly, slowly, and simply. State the problem first: for example, "There's a prowler in my backyard," "My father is having a stroke," or "There's a fire in my kitchen." Then say your address, including the words *street, avenue, drive, boulevard, road*, etc. and your apartment number. Be sure to spell any difficult names. The person you speak to will probably ask your name and phone number and may also ask you to stay on the line (not hang up the phone).

True or False?

Answer *true* or *false*; then correct the false statements. Read aloud the sentences in the passage that led you to your answers.

1. An operator can connect you to emergency services more quickly than if you dial 911.

2. It's a good idea to have the direct numbers of the emergency services pasted on your phone.

3. In the United States and Canada, people have to pay for police, fire, and paramedic services every time they use them.

4. When you call 911, you have to hang up the telephone as soon as you give all the important information.

Vocabulary

Guess the meanings of the underlined words from the contexts. Then match them with the definitions that follow. Write the letters of the definitions in the parentheses.

1. Fen-Lan woke up and thought she heard a <u>prowler</u> (____) downstairs, but it was just her brother making a sandwich in the kitchen.

2. Don't be surprised if you forget all your English in an <u>emergency</u> (____). Just dial the proper service and say "Help!" Then give your address.

3. Practice fire drills in your house so that if there is a real fire everyone will respond <u>automatically</u> (____).

4. If you want to avoid having a heart attack or a <u>stroke</u> (____), you should stop smoking, eat less salt, and exercise more.

5. <u>Paste</u> (____) emergency numbers on the telephone and practice dialing the numbers so that in case of an emergency you will <u>react</u> (____) quickly and correctly.

Definitions

a. a blood clot in the brain that causes death or paralysis (loss of ability to move or difficulty in movement)

b. stick, attach

c. without having to think

d. a sudden, unplanned event requiring immediate action

e. someone who quietly moves around a house or yard looking for something to steal; an intruder

f. to respond to an action or situation

PART B: EMERGENCY SERVICES

Read this passage to yourself quickly. Try to understand new words in context.

The Police: The police deal with problems involving crime, violence, prowlers, robberies, murder, family arguments, noisy neighbors, etc. You should feel free to call the police at any time. State what the problem is; if it is not a police matter, they will tell you who to call.

The Fire Department: Firefighters take care of fires, chemical spills, getting children out of locked rooms, etc. Sometimes they will even get a cat out of a tree!

Paramedics: Paramedics are also called "emergency rescue technicians." Often they are a part of the fire department; sometimes they are a separate public service agency. They are medically trained workers who give first aid to people who have had heart attacks or strokes, or who have nearly choked, drowned, etc. Like the police and fire departments, their services are free. If they have to transfer a sick person to a hospital, however, they will charge for the use of their ambulance service to the hospital.

The Gas Company: If you smell gas at any time, day or night, first check your stove, furnace, and water heater to see if the pilot lights are on. If they are, and you still smell gas, call the gas company immediately. Do not light any matches or cigarettes while waiting for them to come! Open all your windows. Be careful not to create static electricity (small sparks from rubbing one thing against another, such as shoes on carpets).

The Electric Company: If you ever see power lines that have fallen in the street, do *not* touch them or come into contact with any water near them. You could be electrocuted. Call your electric company immediately and report a "downed line."

Remember, these services are available—free of charge—24 hours a day, 365 days a year. Emergencies don't go on vacation; neither do the police or fire departments, paramedics, or power companies.

True or False?

Answer *true* or *false*; then correct the false statements. Read aloud the sentences in the passage that led you to your answers.

1. If the fire department puts out a fire in your kitchen, they will send you a bill.

2. You should try not to embarrass yourself by calling the police if you're not sure a situation is an emergency; just wait and see.

3. Paramedics do not charge for medical services in your home or on the street.

4. If you see a fallen power line, you should try to fix it yourself before you call the electric company.

Vocabulary

Guess the meanings of the underlined words from the contexts. Then match them with the definitions that follow. Write the letters of the definitions in the parentheses.

1. The services of <u>trained</u> (___) people are for the use of <u>the public</u> (___). You should <u>feel free</u> (___) to make use of them in any emergency.

2. Thousands of young children <u>drown</u> (___) or <u>choke</u> (___) to death each year in horrible household accidents.

3. Turning the <u>pilot light</u> (___) of your furnace off in the summer will reduce your gas bill.

4. If you use an electric hair dryer in the bathtub, you might get <u>electrocuted</u> (___).

5. Putting butter or toothpaste on burns is dangerous. No matter what your grandmother taught you, the only safe <u>first aid</u> (___) for a burn is clean, cold water. If the burn is bad, see a doctor immediately.

Definitions

a. be comfortable

b. skilled, knowledgeable, having a lot of practice

c. people in general

d. hurt or killed by electricity

e. die from taking in water instead of air

f. immediate treatment someone gives to an injured person before the doctor arrives

g. stop breathing because something is blocking the air passage

h. a small flame that burns continuously in a gas stove or heater

Discussion Questions

Discuss these questions with your classmates.

1. Describe the police in your country. What do they do?

2. What are the firefighters like in your country?

3. Do you have paramedics in your country? Describe their services.

4. Have you ever been involved in an emergency in your country or here? What happened?

SECTION 2
Emergency Situations

SITUATIONS

Discuss these situations with your classmates. Choose the best
answer, in your opinion. Then compare your answers with the cultural
notes that follow.

1. Nancy Liu was driving to a party. She wore her grandmother's gold
   necklace and her mother's diamond bracelet. On the way, she ran
   out of gas on a deserted street. While she was walking to a phone,
   a man stopped her, took out a gun, and demanded her jewelry.
   What should she have done?
   a. She should have screamed for help.
   b. She should have fought the gunman.
   c. She should have given the gunman her jewelry immediately.

2. Grigor Grigorivich smokes two packs of cigarettes a day. He often
   smokes in bed. He doesn't like to use a smoke detector (a device
   that makes a loud noise when there is smoke in a room) because it
   makes noise when he cooks. What should he do?
   a. Put a smoke detector in the bedroom or as far from the kitchen
      as possible.
   b. Buy a fire extinguisher.
   c. Give up smoking.
   d. a, b, and c.

3. José and María Flores live in the apartment just above Grigor's. At
   3:00 A.M. their smoke detector sounded the alarm. They reacted
   automatically by rolling out of bed and crawling on the floor to
   their closed bedroom door. José felt the door with the back of his
   hand. It was cool, so they slowly opened it and saw smoke coming
   under the front door. Their two daughters had already run out the
   back door. They rushed to a neighbor's house to call the fire
   department. Which actions were correct and why?
   a. None of them were correct.
   b. All of them were correct.
   c. The parents did the right things, but the daughters were wrong.

4. Nicole Sterescu lived alone. She never pulled down her shades at
   night. She was proud of being single and had her full name on the

mailbox. One evening the doorbell rang. A nice-looking man in a suit, carrying a briefcase, politely asked to speak to "Miss Sterescu." He wanted "only a minute of her time to discuss insurance." He had an honest face, so she invited him in. He spoke pleasantly for a few minutes, then opened his briefcase, took out a knife, and raped her. She might have prevented this by:

a. having good locks on her door
b. keeping her curtains drawn and not putting her full name on her mailbox
c. running out of the apartment screaming "Help!"

CULTURAL NOTES

1a. Screaming might have helped, but on a deserted street, even if people heard her, they might not have helped her. In fact, screaming could have made the gunman angrier. Nancy should have checked her gas gauge before leaving her house, and she should have taken a less deserted street.

1b. Fighting the gunman might have made him angry enough to kill her!

1c. It is always a good idea to give someone with a gun whatever he or she wants. By not struggling or resisting, the victim has the best chance of survival. Of course, Nancy could have avoided the situation if she had left her jewelry in the car when she went to the phone. It's sad to lose something important to you, but sadder still to lose the most important thing—your life. At least Nancy had insurance so she could collect money for the loss of her jewelry.

2a. There are over 2 million fires in the United States every year, and cigarettes cause only a small percentage of them. However, roughly 6,000 people die in fires each year, and over one-fourth of them die in fires caused by smoking—a very high percentage. Smoke detectors increase the chances of surviving a fire by 50 percent. A smoke detector should be in every bedroom and hallway, but not in the kitchen. The nose stays asleep longer than the eyes or ears, so you can't rely on your sense of smell to awaken you if there is a fire.

2b. It's a good idea to keep a small fire extinguisher for grease fires and/or a box of baking soda near the stove. Never put water on a grease fire.

2c. Smoking is not only a fire hazard, but a health hazard as well. If Grigor gives up smoking, his chances of dying from a heart attack or stroke will be greatly reduced.

2d. All three answers—a, b, and c—are correct.

3a. They did everything correctly. See 3b.

3b. Breathing smoke causes 75 percent of the deaths in fires. The other 25 percent are caused by burns, falls, heart attacks, etc. José and María trained themselves and their daughters not to jump up in bed. If the room had been full of smoke, jumping up and breathing the smoke would have made them faint. There's usually an inch of "clean air" on the floor, so just to be safe they crawled in that clean air to the door. They knew that a closed door can keep a fire out of a room for 20 minutes. They also knew that if they opened the door and there were fire in the hallway, the new air would make the fire more intense and bring it into their bedroom. So, José touched the door with the *back* of his hand. If the door were hot, it would have burned his more sensitive palm. He didn't touch the doorknob because hot metal burns.

3c. José and María practiced family fire drills so their daughters knew to get out of the apartment immediately without waiting for their parents. Then they all met at a specific place outside to be sure that everyone was safe.

4a. It's important to have good locks, but they work only if you use them. Although the man looked honest, Nicole shouldn't have opened the door. Even if she had just opened it a crack, the man could have easily forced his way in. Not letting the man into her apartment in the first place is the only way Nicole could have avoided trouble.

4b. Because her full name was on the mailbox, Nicole was announcing that she was a single woman. "N. Sterescu" was all that she needed. Of course, by not closing her shades at night, people could see that she was a woman living alone. Whether you are a man or woman, living alone or in a large family, always close your shades or curtains at night so that no one can see in.

4c. If she could have run, she might have escaped. But she was probably paralyzed by fear because the man had a knife. It's nice to know self-defense, but sometimes you can't use it. It's best to avoid a dangerous situation in the first place. (By the way, if you are in a dangerous situation and need help, you might scream "Fire!"; more people respond to that cry than to "Help!" or "Rape!")

A Matter of Life or Death

CALLING FOR HELP

When you use the telephone to call for help in an emergency, you must give all the important information clearly and correctly. Make sure you say what happened, where it happened, and what your name is. Also, unless you have a very common name, it's a good idea to spell it.

Practice these conversations in pairs. Student A is the person who answers the emergency number. Student B describes the problem. Student A should take down the information and check it for accuracy. Then change roles and practice the conversations again. Use different information each time.

Conversation 1

A: Emergency. May I help you?

B: Yes!
- My daughter just swallowed poison.
- My husband is having a heart attack.
- My baby can't breathe.

The address is
- 315 N. Temple Street, Apartment 5.
- 439 Ensenada Avenue.
- 1423 Pine Street.

A: Your name, please.

B: It's
- José Ruiz—R as in *Robert*, U, I, Z as in *zebra*.
- Betty Chu—C, H, U.
- Jaffe—J as in *Jeff*, A, double F as in *Frank*, E.

A: Help is on the way.

Conversation 2

A: Police department.

B: Help! | Someone just robbed my husband.
There's a prowler in my back yard.
Someone stole my car.

The address is | 3333 E. 24th Street, first floor.
539 Taylor.
12604 Gloria Avenue.

A: What's your name?

B: It's | Kim Nguyen—N, G as in *good*, U, Y, E as in *eat*, N.
May Yee—Y, double E.
Sam Sutton—S, U, T, T, O, N.

A: Someone will be right there.

Conversation 3

A: Fire department.

B: | My house is on fire.
There's smoke coming from a window across the street.
My car is on fire.

The address is | 59 Harold Way.
2763 24th Avenue, Apartment A.
6097 Lincoln Boulevard.

A: Your name please.

B: | Rosa Sánchez—S, A, N, C, H, E, Z.
Zoher Chiba—C as in *Charlie*, H, I, B as in *boy*, A.
Michael Hallett—H, A, double L, E, double T.

A: We'll send someone out right away.

Role-play

Read the following situations. If you don't have a 911 emergency number in your community, decide who to call in each case and, if possible, look up the numbers in your local phone book. Then, in pairs, create a conversation for each situation, using your own addresses or inventing addresses. One student answers the emergency number and the other student describes the problem. Then change roles and do the conversation again.

1. It's late. You're in bed. You hear a window break, then footsteps in another room. Who do you call? What do you say?

2. Your elderly neighbor is lying unconscious on the floor. Who do you call? What do you say?

3. You left the kitchen with something cooking on the stove. Now you smell smoke and see flames. Who do you call? What do you say?

Bits and Pieces

PREVENTING EMERGENCIES

In groups of four, read these newspaper stories and discuss how the victims might have prevented these emergencies.

a.

Police found a Chicago woman tied up in the basement laundry room of her apartment building late Monday morning. She said two men attacked her while she was doing her laundry at 5:00 A.M. Apparently no one heard her screams.

b.

Police found a Los Angeles couple dead after a floor heater apparently filled their unventilated apartment with carbon monoxide gas, a spokesman for the sheriff's department said Tuesday. Ten thousand people are hospitalized each year because of carbon monoxide poisoning and 1,500 die from it, he added.

c.

A man hiding behind a bush raped and beat a jogger in Central Park early Wednesday evening. Asked why she didn't blow the whistle around her neck, the jogger said, "I was so frightened that I didn't have enough breath to blow."

d.

A young woman mugged a Brooklyn man late last evening as they rode the same elevator. "Everyone got off at the fifth floor except us. As the door closed, this pretty little thing pulled a gun, grabbed my wallet, hit me on the head, and got out on the eighth floor," Benjamin Shield said from Brourman Hospital.

e.

In Denver, Colorado, a man lost both feet as a result of severe frostbite last Friday. The Los Angeles native was unable to find a motel and slept in his car. Feeling no pain the next morning, he was surprised when a gas station attendant wanted to rush him to the hospital. "I could tell by the way he walked that the boy was in trouble," said the Colorado man. "These folks from Southern California just don't know about the cold."

PRACTICING HOME SAFETY

Complete this checklist about home safety. If you check *no* to any question, put the date when you will correct the problem.

	NO	YES	DATE TO BE FIXED
DOORS, LOCKS, AND WINDOWS			
Do you lock your doors and windows at all times (even when you're at home)?			
Do you have safety locks on your windows so they can be opened, but not all the way?			
Do you have heavy deadbolt locks on all doors, especially glass and screen doors?			
Do you hide extra keys in a safe place (not under the doormat or in a mailbox)?			
Do you have an extra set of keys so you don't need your telephone number or address on your key ring?			
Do you keep ladders inside at night? Do you keep bushes around your windows trimmed?			
Do you close your shades at night?			
VALUABLES			
Before you go out, do you make sure your wallet is in an inside pocket or that your purse is zipped shut?			
Do you hide your valuables in a safe place (not in the sugar bowl or under the mattress)?			
Do you have the serial numbers of your valuables so you can claim them if they are stolen?			
PERSONAL SAFETY			
Do you remove toys and other things from stairways and the middle of rooms?			
Do you clearly mark poison and medicines and keep them out of the reach of children?			
Are you careful not to touch water when you use an electrical appliance?			
Do you check the gas, oil, and water of your car before you drive it?			

KNOWING YOUR ENVIRONMENT

Match the pictures with the advice that follows.

_____ 1. Run for cover, preferably underground, if a tornado is approaching. If there's time, open the windows of your house.

_____ 2. If the lights go out, check the switches or fuses (be sure to have spares). Don't use too many appliances on one circuit.

_____ 3. If you're inside during an earthquake, stay inside. Stand under the archway of a door; turn away from glass. If you're outside, run into the middle of the street, but if there are trees or poles, run into a doorway. Never put your bed under a bookcase, heavy picture, or glass.

Note: Just to be safe, always keep extra water, food, first aid equipment, a manual can opener, a transistor radio, and flashlights in your house.

_____ 4. Turn off the gas immediately if you think there is a leak—or after a tornado or earthquake.

_____ 5. Drink a lot of water, wear a hat, use a good sun block, and avoid hard work or exercise when it is very hot and/or humid.

_____ 6. Put on layers of cotton and wool clothing, gloves, heavy socks and boots, and a hat when you go outside in cold weather. Keep dry. If your fingers or toes become white, hard, and numb (with no feeling), you could be suffering from frostbite. Warm them slowly—first in cool water and then in warm.

Discussion Questions

Discuss these questions with your classmates.

1. Do you know how to turn your gas off? Why is it important to know how to turn it off?

2. If your electricity goes off, what might be the cause?

3. Has the electricity ever gone off where you live now? What did you do?

4. Do you know how to turn your water off? Why is it important to know how to turn it off?

5. What problems might you have in very cold or very hot weather? What can you do to avoid these problems?

6. Are earthquakes or tornadoes a problem where you live now or in your country? If so, when did one last occur? Were you living there then? What did you do?

OPEN-ENDED ACTIVITIES

Choose one or more of the following activities to do outside of class. When you finish, tell the class what you've learned.

1. Visit your local fire department and talk to the firefighters. Read the literature they give you on fire safety and report back to the class.

2. Visit your local police station and talk to the officers. Ask if they have classes in self-defense or if they sell "shriek alarms," small devices that make a loud noise.

3. Take a class in self-defense from your local police officers or somewhere else.

4. Take a CPR class from the fire department, American Red Cross, or Heart Association.

5. Look at the front of your telephone book and see if it has information on first aid.

CHAPTER 4

Community Services

Look at these pictures. Think (in English) about what you see. Study the words and talk about the scenes.

Drivers must:
1. obey the laws
2. purchase insurance
3. have a license

When using public transportation, you may need:
4. a timetable, or schedule
5. a bus transfer
6. a bus token

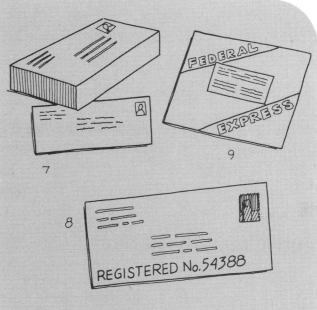

Some ways to send packages are:
7. by first-class mail or parcel post
8. by registered mail
9. by United Parcel Service (UPS), Federal Express, or other private companies

Some city services or facilities are:
10. recreation centers
11. libraries
12. parks

53

Transportation and Public Agencies

PART A: TRANSPORTATION

Read this passage to yourself quickly. Don't worry if you don't know all of the words. Just try to understand them in context.

There are many ways of getting from one place to another in a big city. Depending on the city and how much money you have, you can take a bus, the subway, a taxi, or a streetcar. You might prefer a motorcycle, bicycle, or car. Or you can join the pedestrians and get around on foot.

Taking public transportation may be less expensive than owning your own vehicle. You don't have to worry about buying gas, making repairs, finding a parking place, or getting traffic or parking tickets. And you don't have to purchase automobile insurance, which can be expensive but which is necessary for your own protection.

On the other hand, when you drive your own vehicle, you don't have to worry about transfers, tokens, or timetables. You don't have to wait in the rain for your bus to come, and you can put packages safely in the trunk. With a good map, you can go where you want to when you want to and not get lost.

Whatever method of transportation you choose, be sure you know the traffic and insurance laws of your state. Pedestrians can get tickets for jaywalking, just as drivers can get tickets for breaking the parking and traffic laws.

True or False?

Answer *true* or *false*; then correct the false statements. Read aloud the sentences in the passage that led you to your answers.

1. Only people who drive can get tickets.

2. Taking public transportation may cost you less than driving your own car.

3. Traffic laws are the same throughout the United States and Canada.

4. If you drive a car, you should buy insurance.

Vocabulary

Guess the meanings of the underlined words from the contexts. Then match them with the definitions that follow. Write the letters of the definitions in the parentheses.

1. Pedestrians (___) should wear white at night. They should avoid jaywalking (___) and cross with a green light at a crosswalk instead.

2. When Natasha woke up on the bus, she saw that someone had stolen her purse with her bus pass, bus tokens (___), money, and identification. Fortunately, the bus driver gave her some extra transfers (___), so she could take the next bus home.

3. You need a good map of the city and timetables (___) for the bus and subway so that you can get around efficiently on public transportation.

Definitions

a. walking across the street in the middle of the block rather than at the crosswalk or corner

b. people on foot

c. pieces of paper allowing you to change buses or streetcars without an extra charge

d. pieces of metal used in place of coins for a particular purpose

e. schedules of stops

PART B: PUBLIC AGENCIES

Read this passage to yourself quickly. Try to understand new words in context.

Do you know all the wonderful services available through public agencies? Let's start with the public library, a place where anyone in the community can check out not only books but usually magazines, records, and movies for free. In addition, if you need information on any topic, you can call the reference desk of your central library; the librarian will try to answer your questions or refer you to someone who can.

Another good place to find information is your city councilperson's office. The city council office has brochures explaining all the public services in your area, and people there can answer questions you have about your community.

Be sure to investigate your community and find out what it has to offer. You might be surprised at the number of classes, clubs, recreation centers, parks, museums, lectures, etc., as well as health care and public services that are available to the public free or for a nominal fee.

How can you find out where some of these agencies are? It's easy—by using your telephone book. Your telephone book is filled with useful information, not only on how to use the telephone and what the charges are, but also on how to find government, state, and city offices and other public agencies. In most areas, the telephone book has a special section, usually with yellow pages, to help to find stores, doctors, lawyers, plumbers, etc. And it even has a section on how to give first aid in emergencies!

True or False?

Answer *true* or *false*; then correct the false statements. Read aloud the sentences in the passage that led you to your answers.

1. Library services are expensive.

2. Librarians will answer only questions about books.

3. You might be able to find a free photography class at your local recreation center.

4. City councils deal only with the government; they don't have information about the community.

Vocabulary

Guess the meanings of the underlined words from the contexts. Then match them with the definitions that follow. Write the letters of the definitions in the parentheses.

1. Manuel liked working with people, so he applied for a job at the senior citizen recreation (___) center at the local park.

2. Weera was new to the city and homesick for his native food. His ESL teacher told him that a <u>reference librarian</u> (___) would try to answer any question, so he called and asked where he could find a Thai market. Not only did the librarian tell him, but she spoke clearly and slowly, too.

3. All her life Ionis wanted to go into politics. After law school, she ran for a <u>city council</u> (___) office and the voters elected her. She enjoys working in city government very much.

4. If your books are overdue at the library, you'll have to pay a <u>nominal fee</u> (___) of five or ten cents a day.

Definitions

a. someone in a library who helps people by giving them information

b. a small amount of money you pay for something

c. ways of spending free time that give enjoyment

d. an elected group representing specific parts of the city in the city government

Discussion Questions

Discuss these questions with your classmates.

1. Would you rather drive a car or take a bus? Give reasons for your choice.

2. What community services are available to you where you live? Which of them have you used? Share your information with your classmates.

SECTION 2

Using Community Services

SITUATIONS

Discuss these situations with your classmates. Choose the best answer, in your opinion. Then compare your answers with the cultural notes that follow.

1. Thanh Diem got a puppy. She wants to know if there are any dog obedience classes in her community and where she can get low-cost rabies shots for the dog. She should:
   a. look in the phone book for the number of the animal shelter
   b. call the main library or her city councilperson
   c. do both a and b

2. Rigoberto has just graduated from New York University and is moving back home to Miami. He has a lot of clothes and books—much too much luggage to take on the plane. He should:
   a. have a garage sale
   b. package everything and take it to the post office or send it by United Parcel Service (UPS)
   c. do both a and b

3. Chong Park lives in a big American city. His uncle is buying a new car and giving his old one to Chong. Chong is very excited because he hates riding the bus. There is just one problem—Chong doesn't know how to drive. He should:
   a. teach himself, because it's a simple thing to learn
   b. get a learner's permit and take lessons from a relative, friend, or professional driving instructor
   c. give the car back, because it's too difficult to learn to drive in a big city and owning a car is too expensive

4. Alice Wu gets off work at 12:00 midnight and takes the bus home. She always feels a little afraid. She should:
   a. stand behind the bus bench and hold a gun in her hand
   b. sit as close to the driver as possible
   c. sit with the other passengers and talk to them to keep from feeling lonely

CULTURAL NOTES

1a. The animal shelter—sometimes called the "pound"—or the SPCA (the Society for the Prevention of Cruelty to Animals) or the Humane Society can give Thanh information about rabies shots and dog licenses. It will probably refer her to the department of parks and recreation for information on public dog obedience classes.

1b. The librarian or the city councilperson will probably refer Thanh to the animal shelter or the department of parks and recreation. The librarian can also recommend some books on dog training. The city councilperson can give Thanh a brochure about the city, the district she lives in, and the public agencies in her community.

1c. Both are correct.

2a. If Rigoberto doesn't want to keep his clothes and books, he might make some money by selling them at a garage sale.

2b. He can send his things through the mail or by UPS, depending on what he wants to send and how heavy it is. If he wants to send his things through the post office, he should package his books and clothes separately. The special fourth-class book rate is lower than other rates. He can send clothing and other things regular fourth class (parcel post). It might be cheaper for Rigoberto to pack every-thing in one big box and send it by UPS, depending on the weight of the package and its destination. Rigoberto can find the address and phone number of the nearest UPS office in the phone book. If it is far away, he might want to pay an extra fee for pickup.

2c. Both are correct.

3a. It's not simple to learn how to drive, and a car can be a dangerous weapon in the wrong hands.

3b. Before he does anything else, Chong must pass a written test about driving laws to get a learner's permit. Then he can ask someone to teach him to drive or pay to take private lessons. Chong must be patient and not expect to learn in one day. When he is ready, he must take a driving test at the state department of motor vehicles.

3c. Driving a car is a tremendous responsibility. Chong must learn the laws of his state and be prepared for the expense of insurance. But the freedom a car gives will eventually be very convenient.

4a. It's a good idea to stand behind a bus bench as a protection from cars driving by. Alice should not carry a gun; someone could use it against her. She might want to go to the local police station and buy a "shriek alarm"—a small device that can make an extremely loud noise. She might also want to carry a heavy metal flashlight that she could use to light her way home or as a weapon to protect herself.

4b. The safest place to sit on the bus is as close to the driver as possible.

4c. Even though it's nice to talk to strangers, and it may help improve her English, Alice should be very *unfriendly* at night.

The Post Office and the Telephone

USING THE POST OFFICE

Your local post office has many useful services and items for sale. For instance, you can buy domestic stamps, air-mail stamps, or aerograms. You can send a letter by registered mail or certified mail if you need proof that the right person received it. You can send packages first class or parcel post, depending on how soon you want them to arrive or how much money you want to spend. And you can purchase money orders, which you can use to send money through the mail if you don't have a checking account.

Practice these conversations in pairs. Then fill out the forms.

Conversation 1

CLERK: May I help you?

CUSTOMER: I'd like to send this package to my family.

CLERK: Well, you can send it air mail for—let's see now . . . six dollars and thirty-seven cents.

CUSTOMER: I need to be sure it arrives.

CLERK: Then you can register it if it's valuable, or you could certify it.

CUSTOMER: I'll send it air mail, registered, and I'd like proof of the receipt.

CLERK: Then fill out these forms. On the first form here, just fill out the bottom part, where it says "Customer Completion." On the second form, fill out items one through four. Check box one if you want to know exactly when and to whom the package is delivered. You won't need to check "Restricted Delivery." On item four, check "Registered"—we'll fill in the article number.

CUSTOMER: Okay, thanks very much. Oh, and could I also have two aerograms for overseas letters and a postage rate schedule?

☆ U.S. GOVERNMENT PRINTING OFFICE: 1984 — 756-375

All Entries MUST be in Ball Point or Typed

REGISTERED NO.

POSTMARK OF

Post Office Completion

Reg. Fee $	Special Delivery	$
Handling Charge $	Return Receipt	$
Postage $	Restricted Delivery	$
Received by		☐ Intl

Customer Completion *(Please Print)*

Customer must declare Full value $

☐ With Postal Insurance   ☐ Without Postal Insurance

$25,000 Domestic Ins. Limit

FROM

ZIP CODE

TO

ZIP CODE

PS FORM 3806
July 1983

RECEIPT FOR REGISTERED MAIL *(Customer Copy)*

(See Information on Reverse)

PS Form 3811, July 1983   447-845

DOMESTIC RETURN RECEIPT

● **SENDER:** Complete items 1, 2, 3 and 4.

Put your address in the "RETURN TO" space on the reverse side. Failure to do this will prevent this card from being returned to you. The return receipt fee will provide you the name of the person delivered to and the date of delivery. For additional fees the following services are available. Consult postmaster for fees and check box(es) for service(s) requested.

1. ☐ Show to whom, date and address of delivery.

2. ☐ Restricted Delivery.

3. Article Addressed to:

4. Type of Service:	Article Number
☐ Registered ☐ Insured ☐ Certified ☐ COD ☐ Express Mail	

Always obtain signature of addressee or agent and **DATE DELIVERED**.

5. Signature — Addressee

X

6. Signature — Agent

X

7. Date of Delivery

8. Addressee's Address *(ONLY if requested and fee paid)*

Conversation 2

CLERK: Yes?

CUSTOMER: My family moved recently and we want our mail to come to our new address.

CLERK: Then just fill out this change of address form. Put your name, old address, and new address.

CUSTOMER: What does "Effective Date" mean?

CLERK: The date you want your mail to go to the new address. Put today's date if you have already moved. Do you want to pay a fee to have magazines and newspapers forwarded also?

CUSTOMER: Yes.

CLERK: Then check "yes" in the box on the left. After that, sign and date the form. We'll fill in the boxes on the left at the bottom.

THIS ORDER PROVIDES for the forwarding of First-Class Mail for a period not to exceed 18 months. All parcels of obvious value will be forwarded for a period not to exceed one year.	**Print or Type** (*Last Name, First Name, Middle Initial*)	
CHANGE OF ADDRESS IS FOR: ☐ Firm ☐ Entire Family *(When last name of family members differ, separate orders for each last name must be filed.)* ☐ Individual Signer Only	**OLD ADDRESS** — No. and St., Apt., Suite, P.O. Box, R.D. No. Box	
	Post Office / State / ZIP Code	
I agree to pay forwarding postage for newspapers and magazines for 90 days. ☐ No ☐ Yes	**NEW ADDRESS** — No. and St., Apt., Suite, P.O. Box, R.D. No. Box	
USPS USE ONLY Clerk/Carrier Endorsement	Post Office / State / ZIP Code	
Carrier Route Number	Effective Date	If Temporary, Expiration Date
Date Entered	Sign Here X	Date Signed

☆ U.S. GPO: 1985—469-871

PS FORM 3575, JAN. 1984   *Signature & title of person authorizing address change. (DO NOT print or type.)*

USING THE TELEPHONE

How do you get the number of someone who doesn't live in your area? What are some different ways of making long-distance calls?

Practice these conversations in pairs:

Conversation 1

OPERATOR: Information. For what city, please?

CALLER: Evanston. . . . Ken Mularski on Walnut Grove Avenue: M as in *Mary*, U, L as in *Larry*, A, R as in *Robert*, S as in *Sam*, K, I.

OPERATOR: That's 555-1209.

CALLER: Thank you.

Conversation 2

OPERATOR: May I help you?

CALLER: I'd like to | place a person-to-person call to Ken.
reverse the charges.

OPERATOR: What is your name, please?

CALLER: Barbara.

PERSON ANSWERING: Hello.

OPERATOR: I have a | person-to-person call for Ken.
collect call from Barbara.

Will you accept the charges?

PERSON ANSWERING: | This is Ken.
Yes, of course.

Role-play

Match the situations with the different phone services below. Write the letters in the parentheses. Then, in pairs, play the roles of caller and operator. Have conversations for several of the situations.

    a. Dial 411 for information about local numbers or 1 + area code + 555-1212 for out-of-town numbers.

    b. Dial 0 (operator) and explain the situation.

    c. Dial 0 + the number and place a collect call.

    d. Dial 0 + the number and call person-to-person.

1. (___) Someone has stolen your wallet. You have no money, and you need to call home to have someone pick you up.

2. (___) Your aunt works at Sears in New York. You live in Washington. You need to talk to her, but you know it will take a long time before they can connect you to her department.

3. (___) You can't remember your uncle's phone number.

4. (___) You are talking to your grandmother in Puerto Rico and you are disconnected.

Bits and Pieces

READING TRAFFIC CITATIONS

Andrés Caserta returned to his car one morning after a meeting and found this citation on the windshield. Read the information on the citation, then answer the questions that follow.

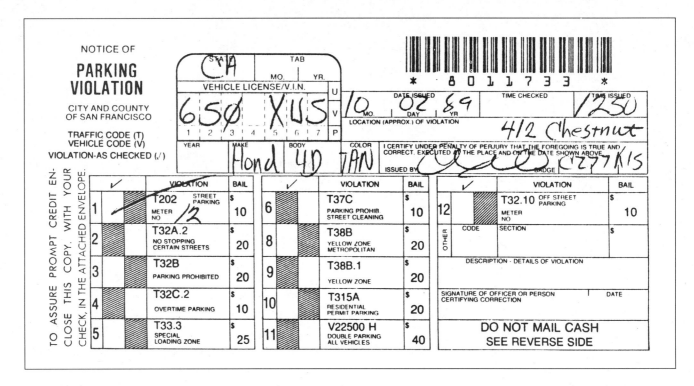

Questions

1. Why did Andrés get the citation? (Another word for *citation* is *ticket*.) That is, what did he do wrong?

2. How much will he have to pay?

3. Where did Andrés get the ticket?

4. Have you ever received a parking ticket? How much did you have to pay?

UNDERSTANDING STREET SIGNS

The following are signs you might see while walking or driving in an American city. The signs on the left have pictures, but no words. The signs on the right have words, but no pictures. Match the signs by drawing lines between them and explain what they mean.

GETTING CAR INSURANCE

If you're going to drive a car, one of the first things you'll have to do is get car insurance. Fill out the following insurance form. Use personal information. If you don't have a car, use information about a car that you know about or one that you would like to have. Ask your teacher for help if necessary.

IMPORTANT — PLEASE COMPLETE ALL INFORMATION

PRESENT INSURANCE CO._____ YEARS INSURED _____ EXPIRATION DATE _____

PREVIOUS INSURANCE CO._____ YEARS INSURED _____ HOW LONG RESIDENT OF CALIF._____
                        (If less than 3 years)

HOME PHONE NO. (_____)_____
                Area Code

BUSINESS PHONE NO.(_____)_____
                   Area Code

MALE ☐   FEMALE ☐

VEHICLE INFORMATION: 467

Car No.	Year	Make	Model (Mustang, Civic, etc.)	Body Style (Station Wagon, 2 Door, etc.)	Auto. or Manual Transmission	Gas or Diesel	Number of Cylinders	Used in Business Other Than To and From Work
1								
2								
3								
4								
5								

NOTE: If truck, camper, or recreational vehicle, give retail cost (new)_____. Length of motorhome or trailer_____.

DRIVER INFORMATION: Married ☐ Single ☐ Widowed ☐ Divorced ☐ Separated ☐ Spouse Licensed: Yes ☐ No ☐

	Names of All Drivers Including Yourself	Relationship	Birthdate Mo.-Day-Yr.	Occupation or Type of Self-Employment	Driver is Principal User of Car No.	Driver is Occasional User of Car No.	Number of Accidents Last 3 Years	No. of Traffic Citations* Last 3 Years	No. of Years Licensed in U.S.A.
1		Self	| |						
2			| |						
3			| |						
4			| |						
5			| |						

*Citation means a moving violation for which you were convicted and fined.

READING MAPS

Most maps have major sites (such as museums, hospitals, and so on) in a list on the back or at the bottom. They also have the streets in the area in an alphabetical list. Next to each location will be a letter and a number. To find the location you want, you can look at the place on the map where the letter and number meet (intersect).

Your instructor will bring in some maps of your area. Work in groups and answer these questions:

1. How would you get from your school to the closest park? From the closest park to the closest hospital?

2. One person in the group names an address (his or her own or someone else's). How would you get from the school to that address?

HUMOR

The following cartoon makes fun of the jaywalking laws in the United States and Canada. Read and discuss it with your classmates.

OPEN-ENDED ACTIVITIES

Choose one or more of the following activities to do outside of class. When you finish, tell the class what you've learned.

1. Visit your city councilperson's office and ask for any brochures that interest you.

2. Call your department of parks and recreation and find out what classes and activities are available.

3. Go to your city animal shelter and find out what services it provides.

4. Go to your local library and get a library card.

5. Go to a museum in your community. Try to find one that has an exhibit on the history of your community.

6. Go to the city zoo and learn the animals' names in English.

CHAPTER 5

Getting a Job

Look at these pictures. Think (in English) about what you see. Study the words and talk about the scenes.

When you apply for a job, you may have to:
1. fill out an application
2. write a resume
3. call for an appointment

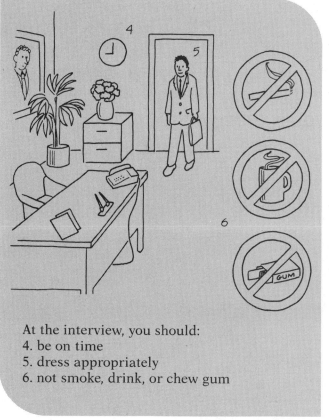

At the interview, you should:
4. be on time
5. dress appropriately
6. not smoke, drink, or chew gum

An applicant can look for a job:
7. in the classified ads
8. at an employment agency
9. by word of mouth

You should consider:
10. the hours of work
11. the salary or wages
12. the fringe benefits

SECTION 1

Finding Employment

PART A: LOOKING FOR A JOB

Read this passage to yourself quickly. Don't worry if you don't know all of the words. Just try to understand them in context.

Because there are often more highly qualified applicants than there are jobs, getting a good job is not easy. It's hard to find a job if you don't have experience, but you can't get job experience without first finding a job!

To find a good job, you must first decide what you are qualified for and what you want to do. You must be realistic. For example, you may *want* to be a computer operator, but unless you have the appropriate training and experience, it is unlikely that you could get that kind of job in the United States or Canada. In addition, the less English you speak, the smaller your chance of getting a good job. So, you may need to get not only job training and experience, but also additional language instruction. If you take a job where everyone speaks your native language, you won't improve your English, and you may have fewer job opportunities in the future.

After you have decided what kind of position you want, look at the "Help Wanted" or "Employment Opportunities" ads in the classified section of your newspaper. These are usually listed alphabetically. The job type or title appears first, often in darker type than the rest of the ad. Job ads may also include how much experience you need, whether the position is full or part time, and what you should do if you are interested in applying (write a letter, call, etc.). You can also go to employment agencies if you need extra help. Agencies, however, usually charge a fee. Try to find one that charges the *employer*, not the *employee*. In addition, make sure you tell all your friends and neighbors that you are looking for a job. You never know who might have an aunt or a cousin who needs someone just like you!

Be prepared to work hard *before* you get the job; you'll spend long hours and lots of energy just *finding* the job. It shouldn't be expensive, though. Since word of mouth has always been free, the dollar you spend on the Sunday newspaper for the classified ads is the only expense you should have when you start to look for a job.

70

True or False?

Answer *true* or *false*; then correct the false statements. Read aloud the sentences in the passage that led you to your answers.

1. You can probably get a good job in the United States or Canada even if you don't speak English.

2. Some employment agencies don't charge the employee; they charge a fee to the employers who hire the applicants.

3. Looking for a job by word of mouth is a waste of time.

4. Employers advertise for employees in the classified ads.

Vocabulary

Guess the meanings of the underlined words from the contexts. Then match them with the definitions that follow. Write the letters of the definitions in the parentheses.

1. Although he had been a doctor in Cambodia, Deth Pran was realistic (___). He knew his English wasn't good enough to pass the state tests, so he applied for a job as a hospital orderly, which he had heard about by word of mouth (___).

2. Most employment agencies (___) are free to employees, but some are not. Be sure they don't charge a fee (___) for their services.

3. A willingness to learn and a pleasant personality are often just as important as actual job experience (___).

4. The classified section (___) of the newspaper is always thickest on Sunday because there are so many "Help Wanted" ads.

Definitions

a. knowledge or skill that comes from practice rather than books

b. concerned with what is practical, able to face the truth

c. through conversation, not writing

d. part of the newspaper that contains announcements about job opportunities, cars for sale, real estate, etc.

e. businesses that place people in jobs

f. money you pay for something

PART B: INTERVIEWING FOR A JOB

Read this passage to yourself quickly. Try to understand new words in context.

After you learn about an available job, you can ask for an interview. When you telephone for an interview appointment, speak clearly and slowly. If your pronunciation isn't good yet, you might want to explain that you are just learning English. It may help to write down what you are going to say and practice it several times before making the call.

Before going to the interview, write a resume of your education and your job experience. An employer doesn't want an autobiography, but organizing information about your qualifications in a resume will help you fill out the application form and answer the interview questions more easily.

Dress well for the interview. Be on time and try to "put your best foot forward." Remember, you probably won't get a second chance, so you want your first impression to be a good one. Be sure to smile and maintain good eye contact with the interviewer.

At the interview, you might want to ask these questions, if the information was not in the advertisement for the job:

1. What are the specific hours, duties, and responsibilities of the position?

2. What is the salary?

3. What are the chances for advancement in the company?

However, don't tell the interviewer that:

1. you move frequently

2. you have many personal problems and life is unfair to you

3. you have changed jobs often

4. you plan to keep this job for only a short time

If you get the job, be sure to find out about the fringe benefits: vacation pay, sick leave, health insurance, etc. Find out how much money for taxes and unemployment insurance the employer will deduct from your salary.

Even if you don't get the position, look on the bright side. You know more about job hunting, you've had a lesson in practical English, and you may get the next job you apply for.

True or False?

Answer *true* or *false*; then correct the false statements. Read aloud the sentences in the passage that led you to your answers.

1. It may be helpful to practice what you will say before you call for an interview appointment.

2. If you make a big mistake at the interview—dress inappropriately

or arrive late—don't worry. You can try the same company again the next week.

3. If you don't get the job after the interview, you have wasted your time.

4. If you have a lot of personal problems, it is a good idea to tell the interviewer about them.

Vocabulary

Guess the meanings of the underlined words from the contexts. Then match them with the definitions that follow. Write the letters of the definitions in the parentheses.

1. If you're looking for a job, you may want to write down all your experience in a <u>resume</u> (___). Even if you don't need a resume, the list of your experience will help you fill out the job application.

2. Although the <u>salary</u> (___) may be lower, some jobs offer good <u>fringe benefits</u> (___), such as long paid vacations, sick leave, free parking, health and life insurance, etc.

3. An employer isn't interested in a long <u>autobiography</u> (___); he or she only needs information about your education and work experience. You need to show that you have the right <u>qualifications</u> (___) for the job.

4. Going to an interview is like meeting your mother-in-law for the first time; the first impression is important. <u>Put your best foot forward</u> (___) by being on time and dressing well.

Definitions

a. a brief written summary of what you have accomplished in your education and jobs

b. payment other than salary or wages made to an employee

c. do the best you can

d. the story of your life that you write

e. weekly or monthly pay

f. experience and ability

Discussion Questions

Discuss these questions with your classmates.

1. What jobs have you had in the past?

2. Do you have a job now? What is it? How did you get it?

3. Have you ever used the classified ads or an employment agency to get a job? If so, describe your experiences.

4. What experiences have you had in job interviews? Describe them.

5. What employment benefits have you had or do you have now?

Translating Your Job Experience into English

SITUATIONS

Discuss these situations with your classmates. Choose the best answer, in your opinion. (There may not be any one correct answer.) Then compare your answers with the cultural notes that follow.

1. María García is 55 years old. She has spent the last 40 years of her life raising children, preparing three meals a day, shopping, and cleaning house. She has just moved here and needs a job desperately. She feels qualified to do housework or baby-sitting, but she would prefer to cook in a Mexican restaurant. She sees an ad in the classified section and calls for an interview appointment. She arrives exactly on time, is clean and neat, and hides her nervousness with a lovely smile. When the interviewer asks María for her job history she should say:
   a. "I've just been a housewife for 40 years."
   b. "I've owned and operated my own restaurant, Casa María, for the past 20 years."
   c. "I have been preparing home-style Mexican cooking for 40 years."

2. Tu Van Nguyen, a refugee from Vietnam, was a bookkeeper there before the war. He was captured while trying to leave and was in prison for 18 months before he was able to escape to America. A friend told him about a job opening at a bank. On the application Tu read, "Have you ever been in prison? If yes, explain." Tu should:
   a. answer *no*
   b. answer *yes* with no explanation
   c. answer *yes* with an explanation that he was a political prisoner

3. For ten years, Arman Bokhasian was a mathematics professor at the University of Yrevan, Armenia. When he applied for his exit visa to the United States, the university fired him. He worked as a janitor for the next three years until the government permitted him to emigrate. Now in Chicago, he places an ad in the newspaper under "Jobs Wanted," and a private school offers him an interview

for a position as a math teacher. At the interview, Arman has to fill out an application asking for "job history, last job first, dates of employment, and reasons for leaving." He should:

a. accurately list both of his past jobs with the dates of employment and reasons for leaving
b. list only his university job, claiming he quit recently to come to the United States
c. list both jobs, reversing the order

4. Fong Kit Lee is from Taiwan. She is very attractive and speaks English quite well. She types 70 words per minute, knows shorthand, and can use computers. She was a secretary for an American company in Taiwan for five years. An employment agency sends her to an interview for a secretarial position. The salary is quite good and Fong knows there is competition for the job. She arrives on time and is well dressed. She smiles at the interviewer and has good eye contact. When the interviewer asks her how she can be an asset to the company, Fong smiles shyly, bows her head, and quietly says she will be happy with the job. The interviewer hires someone else because:

a. Fong's modesty does not impress him
b. the employer sees from her resume that her qualifications are too high; he doesn't want to pay a high salary so he hires a beginner
c. the employer knows that she has never worked in the United States before and doesn't want an inexperienced secretary

CULTURAL NOTES

1a. María should not apologize for being "just a housewife." Instead, she should put her best foot forward and describe her duties in the home in a positive way relevant to the job of "cook" (see 1c).

1b. Claiming she owned a restaurant is "bending the truth" a little too much. She might get the job, but if her employer discovers that she lied, she might get fired. Then María might find it difficult to find another job.

1c. María has done most of the things necessary for running a restaurant. She budgeted for the food, shopped, and planned menus for many years. Her specialty is home-style Mexican cooking, and she is certainly experienced in that. By describing her qualifications in this positive way, she has a good chance of getting the job.

2a. For the past 350 years, America has offered immigrants the chance to start a new life. Tu was arrested seeking freedom, not for dishonesty, theft, or murder. The euphemism for prison in his language is "relocation camp." It's a personal detail of his past life that he doesn't have to mention to anyone.

2b. Even if Tu tries to explain that the prison wasn't really like prisons here, the employer might not be able to hire him because of general bank policy. If he gives no explanation, the bank surely would not hire him.

2c. The employer may or may not understand the politics of the situation; his or her own political opinions might influence Tu's job chances.

3a. You must be honest on a job application. You should, though, emphasize your positive qualifications and experience and de-emphasize or omit the negative ones. Some employers will understand the politics of other countries. The fact that Arman accepted a less important job for reasons of necessity may be a point in his favor.

3b. The employer will probably not be able to check the accuracy of Arman's job history. However, if he lies on the application, he may have trouble later on.

3c. Employers usually prefer applicants who "work their way up" in their careers. In this case, a change from janitor to instructor might give a positive impression, but it would be untrue.

4a. Many cultures stress the importance of humility and modesty. In the United States, however, these qualities are not as important as in some cultures. While North Americans don't approve of conceit, they do talk about their good qualities in a job interview. Because this is difficult for Fong, she should write down all her good points—her assets—before she goes to the interview. If she memorizes them, then when the employer asks her to talk about herself and her qualifications, she can forget what her grandmother taught her, take a deep breath, and discuss her job assets.

4b. Although the company probably doesn't turn Fong down for this reason, in some cases it is a good idea for an applicant to omit some of his or her qualifications.

4c. Fong should put her best foot forward and tell the employer about her experience working for an American company and say that her reliability, enthusiasm, intelligence, self-motivation, and ability to work long hours will make her an asset to the company.

The Job Interview

CALLING FOR AN INTERVIEW

Often an ad says to call for an interview appointment. That first call is very important. If you don't speak well, or if your English is unclear, the person talking to you may simply tell you "the job is already filled," and you won't even get a chance to have an interview in person. You might want to write out what you want to say and practice it before you make the call.

Practice this conversation in pairs. Change roles and use different information each time.

SECRETARY: Good morning.
| Brown and Company.
| Smith's.
| Law offices.

APPLICANT: Hello.
| This is Alicia Romero.
| This is Labib Arafat.
| My name is Zenobia Gyros.

I saw your ad for a
| part-time cook
| bookkeeper
| secretary

| in this morning's *Times*.
| in last evening's *Outlook*.
| on the bulletin board.

I was a
| cook
| bookkeeper
| secretary

in
| Spain
| Syria
| Greece

for
| seven
| two
| ten

years.

I'd like to apply for the job.

SECRETARY:
| I'll connect you with
| You must speak to
| Let me get

| Mr. Gaines.
| Mrs. Richter.
| Ms. Baldaro.

| Please hold.
| Hang on.
| Just a second.

APPLICANT: O.K. Thank you.

77

MAKING AN APPOINTMENT

Often you will have to repeat what you have said many times until you are connected to the right person.

Practice this conversation in pairs. Change roles and use different information each time.

EMPLOYER: We will be interviewing | tomorrow <br> next Thursday
 Tuesday | from 8:00 to 4:00.

I have an appointment open at | 10:45.
 12:15.
 4:45.

Can you | make it then?
 come at that time?

APPLICANT: Yes, I can, | sir.
 ma'am.

EMPLOYER: Good. Bring your resume and come to

843 S. Grand Avenue, Suite 201 | at 10:45
 1320 E. 14th Street, Room 2 | at 12:15
 22 ½ D Drive | at 4:45

tomorrow.
 next Thursday.
 Tuesday.

APPLICANT: That's | 843 S. Grand Avenue, Suite 201
 1320 E. 14th Street, Room 2
 22 ½ D Drive

at 10:45 | tomorrow?
 at 12:15 | next Thursday?
 at 4:45 | Tuesday?

EMPLOYER: That's right.

APPLICANT: Could you please tell me the major cross streets?

EMPLOYER: Sure. We're | on the south side of the street <br> on the north side of the street <br> in the middle of the block

between | 9th and Wilshire.
 Sunset and Figueroa.
 Twain Lane and Clemens Court.

APPLICANT: Thank you. | I'm looking forward to meeting you.
 See you next week.
 I'll see you Tuesday.

EMPLOYER: Good-bye.

TALKING ABOUT YOURSELF

Be sure to write down the time and address of the interview. You may ask for the cross street and about parking, but don't ask for detailed directions or what bus to take. You probably won't be hired if you seem helpless.

Practice this conversation in pairs. Change roles and use different information each time.

INTERVIEWER: Well, | Mr. Kim,
| Mrs. García,
| Ms. Rempe,

you are applying for the position of

| salesman | | store.
| chef | for our | restaurant.
| manager | | company.

Why are you interested in this job?

APPLICANT: I enjoy | selling.
| preparing food.
| working with people.

I'm interested in | fashion.
| Mexican cuisine.
| business.

And I like the challenge this job presents.

INTERVIEWER: What experience do you have to qualify you for this job?

APPLICANT: I've worked in | sales
| restaurants
| business management

since | 1978.
| 1967.
| graduating from college.

INTERVIEWER: Why do you think you'll be an asset to the company?

APPLICANT: Well, I'm very | hard-working.
| reliable.
| enthusiastic.

I take my job seriously and do the best I can.

I'm | always on time
| never sick
| full of energy

and I get along well | with customers.
| fellow workers.
| clients.

INTERVIEWER: You were born in | Korea.
Honduras.
East Germany.

Why did you come to this country?

APPLICANT: There is much more opportunity to succeed in this country.

INTERVIEWER: Very well. Is there anything else you would like to add?

APPLICANT: I would like to thank you for taking the time to interview me. I know that I will do an excellent job and that you will be very pleased with me.

INTERVIEWER: Thank you very much. We will be considering all the applicants this week, and you will be hearing from us shortly. Good-bye.

UNDERSTANDING "HELP WANTED" ADS

Read the following ads and the explanation of abbreviations in job ads. Then answer the questions on page 81.

HELP WANTED

a. **Air conditioning installer,** min. 5 yrs. exp. Co. bnfts. Top wages pd. for qual. person. 555-9000

b. **Cook,** NY pizza restaurant, exp. needed. Call Pete, 555-1400.

c. **Driver,** delivery truck. Need license and good dr. rec. 555-1309

d. **Gardener.** No exp. required, will train. Temp./perm. jobs, 555-2400.

e. **Restr. mgr.** Send resume: P.O. Box 77, Ft. Worth, TX.

f. **Restaurant** host/hostess, waiter/waitress, dishwasher. Gd. sal. and xlnt bnfts. Call Jean, 555-6400.

g. **Secretary,** m./f., 2 yrs. exp. nec. Send resume: P.O. Box 588, Houston, TX.

Abbreviations

bnfts. = benefits
co. = company
dr. rec. =driving record
exp. = experience
gd. sal. = good salary
m./f. = male or female
mgr. = manager
min. = minimum
nec. = necessary
perm. = permanent
pd. = paid
qual. = qualified
restr. = restaurant
temp. = temporary
yr./yrs. = year or years
xlnt. = excellent

Questions

Answer these questions. Read aloud the words in the ads that led you to your answers.

1. What jobs might a person apply for if he or she:

    _____   doesn't cook but knows about restaurant management

    _____   has installed air conditioners for the last 12 years

    _____   has no previous experience in any job and likes to work outdoors

    _____   has a good driving record

    _____   has just come from Italy and makes pizza

2. Which jobs ask for resumes? _____

3. Which job ads ask you to call for an interview appointment?

    _____

Role-play

Look at the ads in the preceding exercise or in your local newspaper and find a job offer that interests you. With a partner, role-play a call to ask for an interview. One student will be the job applicant and the other, the employer. After you make the appointment, role-play a practice interview. Then find another job offer and change roles.

Bits and Pieces

WRITING RESUMES

A resume is a brief summary of your experiences and education relevant to the job you are seeking. The following are examples of two types of resumes. Luis Hernández lists his experience *chronologically*. Tuyet Binh Nguyen lists her experience *functionally*. How are they different? Why would you use one type instead of the other?

Luis Hernández
227 E. 27th Street
New York, NY 10009
(212) 055-6527

CAREER OBJECTIVE	A position in restaurant management
EDUCATION	City College, New York City B.S., Business Administration
JOB EXPERIENCE	<u>Head Waiter</u> 3/86 to present Los Siete Mares, Brooklyn Oversee a staff of 15 waiters and busboys, assign stations, make reservations, greet guests, check daily receipts <u>Waiter</u> 1/84-2/86 La Luz del Día Café, Greenwich Village Waited tables in an extremely busy restaurant <u>Cashier</u> 3/82-10/83 Café Moctezuma, Mexico City, Mexico Took all receipts, made change, balanced each day's receipts, made bank deposits
OTHER EXPERIENCE	<u>Cook</u> 1/80-2/82 Para los Niños Day-Care Center, Puebla, Mexico Cooked breakfast and lunch for a children's center; designed menus and made weekly budgets

---

Tuyet Binh Nguyen
3120 Bunker Hill Street
Los Angeles, California   90012
(213) 555-2626

CAREER OBJECTIVE   A position in banking with special interest in
                        real estate loans

EXPERIENCE SUMMARY

  Accounting
        Prepared and supervised profit and loss statement, analyzed
        investment planning, consulted on real estate purchases.
        Designed new and modern accounting procedures.

  Banking
        Advanced from position of cashier to teller to assistant manager.
        Designed development of merchant account department.

  Real Estate
        Passed California real estate sales examination and sold five
        houses in the first month. Assisted in development of business
        sales office and sold two businesses in two months.

EMPLOYERS

  Fu Ling Real Estate Company   1987 to present
  Los Angeles, California

  East-West National Trust   1979-1985
  Hong Kong

  Pearl of the Orient Exports   1970-1974
  Saigon, Vietnam

EDUCATION

  UCLA Extension classes in English as a second language, accounting,
  BASIC computer language   1986-1988

  Anthony Real Estate Schools   1986

  Saigon University, major in economics   1968-1970

References available upon request

WRITING THE COVER LETTER

Always send a brief, positive cover letter with your resume. Read this example. Then write your own resume, either chronological or functional, with a cover letter.

---

227 E. 27th Street
New York, New York 10009
September 6, 19XX

Mr. Albert Smith
Director of Personnel
La Cazuela Restaurants
1323 Madison Avenue
New York, New York 10014

Dear Mr. Smith:

    I am writing in regard to your ad for a restaurant manager in this Sunday's Times. As a college graduate in business administration, with 20 years' experience in the restaurant trade, I am confident that I qualify for the position.

    My fluency in both Spanish and English enables me to speak to workers and guests in their native languages.

    I am eager to meet with you to discuss my qualifications further. I will contact you within a week to see if we can arrange a meeting.

                            Sincerely yours,

                            Luis Hernández

                            Luis Hernandez

FILLING OUT JOB APPLICATIONS

Practice filling out this job application. (When you are filling out a real one, try to get two copies of the form so you can fill out one and correct your mistakes, then fill out the other perfectly.)

APPLICATION FOR EMPLOYMENT

DATE _____

Position Applied For _____ Referred By _____

PERSONAL

Name _____ Phone (_____) _____

Present Address _____
No.   Street   City   State   Zip

Social Security No. _____

In case of emergency, notify _____ Phone (_____) _____

Are you 18 years old or over?   Yes_____ No_____   (If employed and you are under 18 years of age, a work permit may be required.)

Are you a U.S. citizen or do you have the legal right to work in the U.S.? _____ (If not a citizen, you will be required to furnish proof of your legal right to remain and work permanently in the U.S.)

If hired, on what date will you be available to start work? _____

List any relatives you have presently employed by this company. _____

Have you ever been convicted of a felony?   Yes_____ No _____ If so, indicate number of convictions. _____

Do you have any physical condition which may limit your ability to perform the job applied for? _____
_____

(Offer for employment may be made contingent on passing a physical examination.)

EMPLOYMENT RECORD

List present or most recent employment first. If lapses occurred between periods of employment, give dates and reasons for unemployment

Company _____ Job Title _____

Address _____ Phone (_____) _____

Dates Employed _____ To _____ Salary _____

Supervisor's Name & Title _____

Reason for Leaving _____

May we contact this employer? _____

Company _____ Job Title _____

Address _____ Phone (_____) _____

Dates Employed _____ To _____ Salary _____

Supervisor's Name & Title _____

Reason for Leaving _____

May we contact this employer? _____

Company _____ Job Title _____

Address _____ Phone (_____) _____

Dates Employed _____ To _____ Salary _____

Supervisor's Name & Title _____

Reason for Leaving _____

May we contact this employer? _____

Company _____ Job Title _____

Address _____ Phone (_____) _____

Dates Employed _____ To _____ Salary _____

Supervisor's Name & Title _____

Reason for Leaving _____

May we contact this employer? _____

EDUCATION BACKGROUND

Type of School	Name & Location	How Many Years	Graduated Yes	No	Course or Major
HIGH SCHOOL					
TRADE OR BUSINESS					
COLLEGE					
OTHER					

BUSINESS SKILLS

Office Applicants:
  What office machines can you operate? _____

_____

  Typing: Words per minute? _____ Dictation: Words per minute? _____

Plant Applicants:
  What machines can you operate? _____

_____

Restaurant Applicants:
  List the various jobs you have held in restaurants. _____

ADDITIONAL INFORMATION

  Have you served in the U. S. Armed Forces? Yes ___ No ___

  What foreign languages do you speak? _____

  What foreign languages do you write? _____

List any additional information not already shown which you feel would be helpful to us in considering you for employment.

_____

_____

I hereby certify that the statements made by me on this application for employment are true and correct, and that if anything I have entered hereon is found to be untrue. I may be subject to discharge.

_____   _____
      Applicant's Signature   Date

Office Use Only

Interviewed by _____ Date _____

OPEN-ENDED ACTIVITIES

Choose one or more of the following activities to do outside of class. When you finish, tell the class what you've learned.

1. Find two or three ads for the same kind of job in the classified section of the newspaper. Compare the job offers. Which one offers the most money? Which one looks the most interesting?

2. Call an employment agency and get information about their services.

3. Answer an ad in the paper and ask for information about the job.

4. Talk to people who have jobs that interest you. Ask how they got their jobs.

CHAPTER 6

Minding Your Money

Look at these pictures. Think (in English) about what you see. Study the words and talk about the scenes.

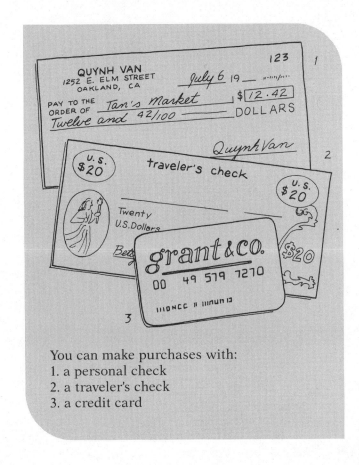

You can make purchases with:
1. a personal check
2. a traveler's check
3. a credit card

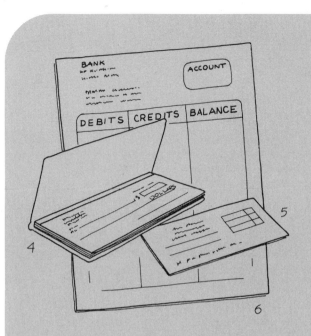

With a checking account, you will get:
4. a checkbook
5. deposit slips
6. a monthly statement

If something won't work when you get it home, you should:
7. take it back and ask for a refund or exchange
8. take your receipt as proof of purchase

You can shop for bargains at:
 9. garage sales
10. discount stores

89

SECTION 1
Your Money

PART A: PROTECTING YOUR MONEY

Read this passage to yourself quickly. Don't worry if you don't know all of the words. Just try to understand them in context.

There is a saying in English that "money is the root of all evil," but most people in fact love money, enjoy spending it, and think that not having *enough* money is the real evil. We all work hard to make money; therefore, we should keep it in a safe place or spend it wisely.

A bank account is one way of keeping your hard-earned money safe—keeping it at home is *not* safe. Because so many people do hide their money at home—under a mattress or in the sugar bowl—burglars often look in obvious hiding places first. Even if you are lucky enough never to be robbed, if you keep your money at home you run the risk of losing it in a fire or other disaster. The safest place to keep money is in a bank, either in a checking account or in a savings account. You can use the money in a checking account at any time, but there is often a service charge. There are often restrictions on withdrawing money from savings accounts, but your money works for you by collecting interest while you're not using it.

Opening a bank account is not difficult. It's easy to learn how to make a deposit and balance your monthly bank statement so that you don't withdraw more than you should. However, it's embarrassing if a check bounces (is not good because you don't have enough money in your account)—and it is against the law in some places. Be sure to choose a bank that has a low service charge and a good interest rate.

Not only is a checking account safe, but your canceled check is proof that you paid your bill. In most cases, the bank sends you these canceled checks every month with your statement. Also, since it is unsafe to mail cash, checks make bill paying safer and more convenient than paying in person or buying a money order.

Another way to protect your money is by buying traveler's checks. You can buy them at most banks. You don't even have to have an account at the bank where you buy them, but you will probably have to pay a small fee. If these are lost or stolen, the traveler's check company will refund your money.

90

True or False?

Answer *true* or *false*; then correct the false statements. Read aloud the sentences in the passage that led you to your answers.

1. As long as you can find a good hiding place for your money, you don't need to put it in a bank.

2. If you put your money in a savings account, it can earn money for you.

3. You can't buy traveler's checks unless you have a bank account.

4. If someone says you didn't pay your bill when in fact you did, your canceled check from the bank will prove that you paid.

Vocabulary

Guess the meanings of the underlined words from the contexts. Then match them with the definitions that follow. Write the letters of the definitions in the parentheses.

1. While Sam was on vacation, a pickpocket stole his traveler's checks (___). He immediately went to the local office of the traveler's check company and got his money back.

2. Charles was embarrassed. He had just opened a checking account, but he didn't know how to balance (___) his new account and he was afraid a check might bounce (___). A helpful bank officer showed him how to balance the account.

3. The telephone company was threatening to disconnect Phuong's phone for nonpayment. Fortunately her bank statement (___) arrived in time. She made a copy of both sides of the canceled check (___) and sent the copy to the phone company to prove she had paid her bill.

4. Romelia Ibarra opened her first checking account (___) with a deposit (___) of $739.15 from her first paycheck. She then decided to withdraw (___) $39.15 to take her grandmother to dinner.

5. A bank service charge (___) for a checking account can be $7 a month, but it's cheaper than buying money orders.

6. When Ulysses gave up smoking, he put all the money he would have spent on cigarettes into a savings account (___) that paid 7.5% interest (___). At the end of one year, he had saved $387!

Definitions

a. a check that is returned to you with your bank statement after the bank has cashed it

b. a fee for services

c. be returned unpaid because there is not enough money in the account

d. money a bank pays a customer while it keeps (and uses) his or her money

e. checks for a fixed amount that a bank or travel agency sells and that can be cashed in most places

f. a monthly report from the bank with a record of all deposits and withdrawals, service charges, and beginning and ending balances

g. money put into an account

h. a bank account used for the payment of bills and exchanges of money

i. take money out of an account

j. a bank account in which money is put aside for future use and earns interest

k. determine the amount of money going out of and coming into an account

PART B: SPENDING YOUR MONEY

Read this passage to yourself quickly. Try to understand new words in context.

Spending money can be fun if you're careful and follow your budget so you don't spend more than you have. Decide how much you need for your daily living expenses: your rent or mortgage, food, utilities, medical bills, car, etc. Then decide how much you want to save.

After you look at your budget and decide what you can spend on clothes, furniture, etc., you can save a lot if you hunt for bargains. Try to buy name-brand merchandise at reliable discount stores or at sales. Check newspaper ads and store catalogs, or call different stores and ask for the prices of specific items. You will save money by comparison shopping. Also, remember that a high price doesn't always indicate good quality; learn to recognize well-made products so you can get the most for your money.

Most stores in the United States and Canada have sales throughout the year. The best bargains are often at the "month-end" sales in the large department stores. Other sale times are after holidays like Christmas and during the weekends of holidays like Presidents' Day. Stores advertise their sales in local newspapers.

Flea markets, garage sales, and swap meets are bargain hunters' paradises. At these events, people sell their old or unwanted items for low prices. Sometimes you can find some very good buys. What is junk to one person could be a treasure to someone else.

You can usually pay for your purchases with credit cards. Credit cards are convenient and safe because you don't have to carry a lot of cash around with you. This "plastic money" also lets you put off making payments for a month. But be careful with credit cards—don't forget that eventually you will have to pay the bill with real money.

True or False?

Answer *true* or *false*; then correct the false statements. Read aloud the sentences in the passage that led you to your answers.

1. High prices always mean good quality in the United States.

2. Stores have sales only once or twice a year.

3. Items at garage sales are usually new.

4. You can sometimes find the lowest price for an item just by making several phone calls.

Vocabulary

Guess the meanings of the underlined words from the contexts. Then match them with the definitions that follow. Write the letters of the definitions in the parentheses.

1. When Regina Polinski went to a discount store (___) to shop for a color television, she found a Sony set for $350 and a set from a company she had never heard of for only $300. She bought the Sony set because she trusted the name brand (___) more.

2. Jim and Suzanne Prager were such bargain hunters (___) that they spent every Saturday morning going to garage sales (___), and they went to flea markets (___) every Sunday.

3. Buying a new refrigerator was barely within their budget (___), so Mr. and Mrs. Romero did a lot of comparison shopping (___). They were both shocked and delighted to find the model they wanted at a discount store for $210 less than at an appliance store.

4. Mr. Whitney didn't know that the ugly piece of junk (___) he sold for $5 at his garage sale was actually a valuable antique.

5. Zenobia had American Express, Visa, MasterCard, and Diner's Club credit cards (___), but the restaurant would accept only cash.

Definitions

a. people who enjoy looking for good deals and purchasing merchandise for less money than it's worth

b. plastic cards that let people purchase merchandise and pay later

c. a store that sells merchandise for less money than other stores do

d. anything regarded as useless or of little value

e. private sales in which individuals sell items no longer wanted or needed—also called yard sales

f. large markets—usually open-air—where inexpensive items are for sale by different sellers

g. an estimate or plan of income and expenses

h. comparing the price of the *identical* item at many different stores

i. a known manufacturer with a reliable history—for example, Sony, RCA, etc.

Discussion Questions

Discuss these questions with your classmates.

1. Do you have a bank account? If so, tell what happened at the bank when you opened it. (But you don't have to tell how much money you have in it—this is considered personal information in North America.)

2. Do you have any credit cards? If so, which ones and what did you do to get them?

3. In your country, is it safer to hide money at home, spend it, or keep it in a bank? Explain.

4. Do you keep a budget? Describe how you handle your income and expenses.

Saving and Spending Money

SITUATIONS

Discuss these situations with your classmates. Choose the best answer, in your opinion. (There may not be any one correct answer.) Then compare your answers with the cultural notes that follow.

1. Mario Cuadra has been in San Diego for 6 months. He has a good job as a delivery person for a gourmet store. Not only does he make a good salary, but because of his pleasing personality, he gets good tips. He has already saved $2,500 for his college tuition. To protect his money, he should:
   a. hide it in a very safe place in his house
   b. put it in a bank
   c. turn it into traveler's checks

2. Noriko Watanabe is a visa student from Japan. She tried to get a MasterCard but the bank turned her down because she didn't have sufficient credit history. She should:
   a. open an account at a bank that issues MasterCards
   b. try to get a Visa or American Express card instead
   c. first establish credit where it is often easy to get: with a department store, gas station, etc., and then reapply for a major credit card in 6 months

3. Azeb Mamamoudie has just had her third child. Trips to the laundromat are very difficult for her, so by careful budgeting she has saved enough money to buy a washing machine. She should:
   a. buy the cheapest one because she doesn't have a lot of money
   b. research which machine is the best quality, then do comparison shopping or wait until the machine is on sale
   c. buy a used one

4. Mohammed and Turan Sharifi are expecting their first baby in September. They will need a crib, highchair, car seat, stroller, and other necessary items, but they're on a limited budget. They should:
   a. have a "baby shower" and invite all their friends, who will bring gifts
   b. go to a discount store and buy on credit
   c. look for baby furniture at garage sales

5. Juan Balboa put an ad in the newspaper to sell his old car. A man came to see it, made a good offer, and started to give Juan a check. If Juan accepts the check and gives the man the car, the following could happen:
   a. Juan goes to the bank and cashes the check without any problems.
   b. Juan tries to cash the check and finds that the buyer has put a stop payment on it (a stop payment tells the bank not to cash a check), so Juan has no money and no car.
   c. The check bounces and Juan has no money and no car.

6. Priscilla Morales bought an expensive shirt for her husband Thomas. When she washed it, she followed the instructions on the label, but when Thomas put the shirt on again, it had shrunk. She should:
   a. give it to Goodwill Industries
   b. give it to her young son
   c. return it to the store and demand an exchange or a refund

CULTURAL NOTES

1a. There really is no completely safe place to hide valuables in a home. Most burglars are very clever; they look in all the drawers, behind pictures, in the freezer, even inside the toilet tank! And, even if Mario isn't robbed, he could lose all his money in a fire.

1b. Of course, the safest place for Mario to put his money is in a bank. He should make sure that the bank's accounts are insured by the FDIC (Federal Deposit Insurance Corporation). Most banks require only two pieces of identification and a small amount of money to open an account. A bank officer can help Mario decide what kind of account best suits his needs.

1c. Keeping money in a bank in the United States or Canada is very safe, but if Mario's memories of unreliable banks in his country make him too nervous, he can turn his money into traveler's checks. The check will probably cost a fee of one percent—that is, one dollar for every hundred—a small price to pay for safety. He must be sure to keep a record of the numbers of the checks (separate from the checks) so that if the checks are lost, stolen, or destroyed, he will get his money back. Of course, he will not receive interest on his money.

2a. It's hard to get a credit card without having had credit in the past, but how do you get your first card? It helps to have a bank account, and it's a good idea for Noriko to open an account at a bank that issues credit cards. Then she'll have to wait a little while.

2b. Usually, if one major credit card company turns you down, the others will do the same, but it can't hurt to try. (It's easier to get a Visa or MasterCard than an American Express card.) It doesn't cost anything to apply (even the postage is normally paid), and you'll get practice in filling out applications in English!

2c. Noriko has to start to establish a credit history somewhere. After opening a bank account, she should apply for credit cards at department stores such as Sears, J.C. Penney, and Montgomery Ward and gas stations like Shell and Texaco. It is usually fairly easy to establish credit with businesses such as these. To establish credit, she should plan to use the cards often and pay the bills promptly.

3a. Often, the least expensive machine can end up costing the most money in repairs and inconvenience.

3b. Azeb should go the library and use a magazine called *Consumer Reports*. This magazine gives comparative information on the quality of many different products, from cars to toothpaste. She should look first in the index for *Consumer Reports* magazine under the category "washing machines." The index will tell her what issue and page numbers to look for. After she reads the information, she should choose the make and model of the machine she wants and then call different stores to find the least expensive price. She can also wait for a sale.

3c. Buying a used machine is also a good idea. Azeb should still do research on the best-quality machine (see b). She can find used appliance dealers in the yellow pages of the telephone book.

4a. Babies can be very expensive, and often friends and family will help by having a baby shower. Sometimes the hosts or hostesses get together and buy a big gift like a crib or stroller. But Mohammed and Turan shouldn't give the shower themselves. A friend or family member should do it for them.

4b. There are a lot of reliable discount stores where they might get good buys, but baby furniture can be very expensive. If they buy on credit but don't have the cash to pay for it later, they could go into debt.

4c. Garage and yard sales are wonderful places to find good, almost new, baby furniture. Remember, babies grow so fast that people don't use cribs, strollers, etc. very long. Often you can get great bargains on those items, and they'll be just as good as new.

5a. If the man is honest, Juan will have no problem cashing the check. But when you sell something to someone you don't know, it's safer to ask for cash. If you can't get cash, have the buyer give you a "cashier's check" or a certified check. These are printed orders for the payment of money issued by a bank. The buyer has already exchanged the appropriate amount of money for them, so they're safe.

5b. If a checking account holder isn't satisfied with something he or she has purchased, or if the check has been lost or stolen, he or she can instruct the bank to "stop payment" on that check. However, a dishonest person can use this procedure as well to avoid paying for what he or she has just bought.

5c. If there are insufficient funds in the account, the bank will not cash the check. It is illegal to write checks without having enough money in an account, but it might be hard to find the man—or Juan's car. Even worse, if Juan deposits the check in his account and writes checks against this money, Juan's checks could bounce as well!

6a. It is a popular North American practice to give away old clothes to different charities such as Goodwill Industries, the Salvation Army, etc., but Thomas's shirt is too new to give away.

6b. She could give it to her son, but she really should . . .

6c. . . . go back to the store and demand an exchange (although the same thing might happen if she gets the same brand) or a refund of her money. If the salesperson refuses to help her, she should see the manager. If the manager won't help, she should write letters to the president of the store and her local consumer complaint bureau. You'd be surprised at the power of a letter.

Consumer Rights

ASKING FOR A REFUND OR EXCHANGE

Occasionally you spend your hard-earned money on an item in a store, then bring it home and find that there is something wrong with it. In most cases, you have a right to take it back to the store for a refund. Some small shops will only offer an exchange for other merchandise in the store, however. Always save your receipt, but don't hesitate to *try* to return a defective item even if you can't find the receipt.

Practice these conversations in pairs:

Conversation 1

CUSTOMER: I'd like to return this sweater.
SALESPERSON: What seems to be the problem?
CUSTOMER: It has a hole in it.
SALESPERSON: Do you have the receipt?
CUSTOMER: No, it was a gift.
SALESPERSON: I can't refund your money, but I'll exchange it.

Conversation 2

CUSTOMER: I'd like to return this television.
SALESPERSON: Why are you returning it?
CUSTOMER: It doesn't work.
SALESPERSON: But it was on sale "as is."
CUSTOMER: It worked in the store, but it doesn't work now.
SALESPERSON: You'll have to return it to the manufacturer.

Role-play

Work with a partner. One person is a salesperson, and the other is a customer who wants to return something. Role-play the following situations, with the customer having these problems:

The customer:

1. Your mother-in-law gave you a bright green tie for your birthday. You don't wear ties and you hate green.

2. You bought a tape recorder at a discount store; when you got it home, it wouldn't record.

3. You washed a plaid cotton jacket you bought two weeks ago. You followed the instructions, but all the colors ran (it lost its color pattern).

4. You bought a chicken at the supermarket; when you started to prepare dinner, you noticed it smelled bad.

MAKING A COMPLAINT

What should you do if you feel that someone has overcharged you for a service or that you've had to pay for bad service? This can be very frustrating, but the consumer protection agency or Better Business Bureau in your area can help you. You can find the agency's phone number in your telephone book.

Practice these conversations in pairs:

Conversation 1

CONSUMER COMPLAINT
BUREAU OPERATOR: Complaint board.

ANGRY CONSUMER: I'd like to make a complaint.

OPERATOR: What kind of service are you calling about?

CONSUMER: A gas station.

OPERATOR: Please hold on. I'll transfer you.

CLERK: What seems to be the problem?

CONSUMER: Hank's Gas Station on Oak Street charged me for fourteen gallons of gas, but my car holds only ten.

CLERK: I'll send you some complaint forms to fill out. What is your address?

Conversation 2

CONSUMER COMPLAINT
BUREAU OPERATOR: Complaint board.
ANGRY CONSUMER: I'd like to make a complaint.
OPERATOR: What kind of complaint?
CONSUMER: It's about a dentist.
OPERATOR: Please hold on. I'll connect you.
CLERK: What is your complaint about?
CONSUMER: A dentist on Eighth and Main. He filled the wrong tooth.
CLERK: Oh, that's covered by another agency. Let me give you their number.

Role-play

Work with a partner. One person has sold something to or performed a service for the other. Role-play the following situations, with the customer or client having these problems:

1. You went to the beauty parlor or barber shop and asked the stylist to trim your long hair "just a little." The stylist cut it very short and gave you the bill.

2. You took your clothes to the dry cleaner's. When you picked them up, one item was torn.

3. You bought a used washing machine at a garage sale. When you got it home, it didn't work.

4. You went to an optometrist for reading glasses. When you picked them up, you couldn't read with them on. The optometrist orders new glasses but says he will charge you for both pairs.

SECTION 4

Bits and Pieces

SAFETY IN BANKS

Read this article. Discuss it with a partner. Could this happen to you?

Dreams Go Up In Smoke

Fifty-seven-year-old Rosa Miranda was in County Hospital today after an attempted suicide. Yesterday she came home from work to find her apartment in flames. She allegedly lost $20,000 in cash, her life savings, plus some antique jewelry with a value of $7,000. "I begged her to put her money in a bank and the jewelry in a safety deposit box," her thirty-year-old son, Roberto, said. "But she just didn't trust anybody."

OPENING A BANK ACCOUNT

On the following page is an example of the kind of form you have to fill out when you open a bank account. Read the form; the following notes may help you.

Notes

1. **Individual ownership:** just you

2. **Joint tenants:** you and someone else

3. **Please mail or hold all my statements:** Do you want the bank to mail the statements to your home or do you want them to hold them so you can go to pick them up?

4. **Account Name 1:** your name. If other people will share the account, list them under *Account Names 2* and *3*.

BEST SAVINGS
AND LOAN ASSOCIATION

Date _____

REQUEST FOR INTEREST EARNING CHECKING ACCOUNT

I want my account to be: (Please check box desired)

☐ Individual Ownership
☐ Joint Tenants with Right of Survivorship
☐ Individual as Trustee for_____ Beneficiary(s)
☐ Joint Trustee for_____ Beneficiary(s)
☐ Community Property
☐ Tenants in Common
☐ Trustee of Existing Trust
☐ Fiduciary

PLEASE PRINT:

Account Names   1 _____
2 _____
3 _____

Please indicate by number which person's Social Security Number will be used for tax reporting purposes ☐

If joint account, please indicate the number of signatures required to sign or withdraw ☐

Please ☐ MAIL or ☐ HOLD all my statements and other notices (check one). If held, mail them to me if I do not pick them up in 30 days.

I am currently a Silver Circle member. ☐ YES ☐ NO   (check one)

I have selected the following style of 200 personalized checks:

Style _____ Wallet Color _____

PLEASE INDICATE OTHER ACCOUNTS BY NUMBER HELD IN THE ABOVE NAMES.

_____ _____ _____

IDENTIFICATION	Account Name 1	Account Name 2	Account Name 3
SOCIAL SECURITY NUMBER			
BIRTHDATE			
MOTHER'S MAIDEN NAME			
DRIVER'S LICENSE NUMBER			
OTHER IDENTIFICATION			
PHONE NUMBERS Home			
Business			

HOUSEHOLD ADDRESS - street address _____
- city, state, zip _____

MAILING ADDRESS IF DIFFERENT THAN HOUSEHOLD
street address_____
city, state, zip _____

FOR OFFICE USE ONLY

M.M. NUMBER	RELATIONSHIP	SERVICE CLASS CODE	CUSTOMER PROFILE CODE	SAFE KEEPING	OTHER I/D

103

Now fill in the form with information about yourself.

MAKING A DEPOSIT

Look at the filled-in deposit slip and answer these questions.

1. How much currency (cash in bills) is Thomas depositing?
2. How many checks is he depositing? What are the amounts?
3. Thomas wants some money in cash, so it is subtracted from the deposit. How much cash does he take with him?
4. What is the total deposit?

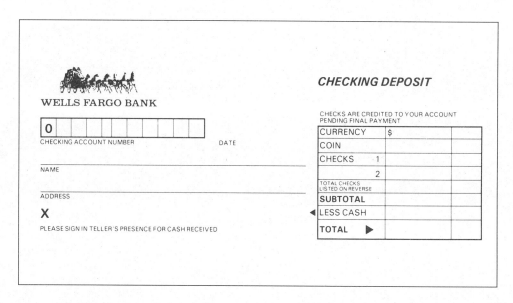

Now fill in the blank deposit slip. You want to deposit two checks, one for $50.25 and the other for $248.19. You want $60.00 in cash.

WRITING CHECKS

Look at the filled-in check below and answer these questions.

1. Who is the account holder (the person who signed the check and whose name is printed on the check)?

2. What is the amount of the check? (Notice that it is written in words as well as in figures.)

3. Who is the check to ("Pay to the order of . . . ")?

4. The account number is the computerized number at the bottom of the check. At the right on the top line is the check number. What is the check number?

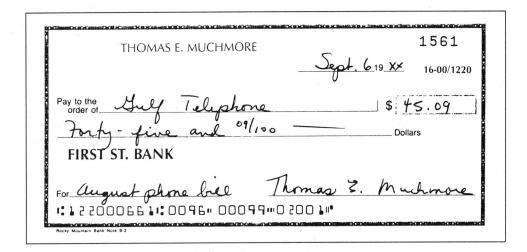

Work with a partner. Use the blank check form to write a check to your partner. One of you should write a check for $213.78, and the other should write a check for $52.90. Don't forget to sign and date the checks. (Note: If these checks were real, you would have to sign them on the back before cashing or depositing them.)

THOMAS E. MUCHMORE   1561

_____19____   16-00/1220

Pay to the
order of_____ $_____

_____ Dollars

FIRST ST. BANK

For_____   _____

⑆12 200066 ⑆: 0096⑈ 00099⑈0 200 ⑈

Rocky Mountain Bank Note B-2

CANCELED CHECKS

Thomas Muchmore received a five-day shut-off notice for nonpayment of his telephone bill. He had paid the bill and had the canceled check. On the back of canceled checks is information about who cashed the check and the date he or she cashed it. What should Thomas do?

a. pay the phone company again immediately

b. send the original canceled check to the phone company to prove he had paid the bill

c. call the phone company and then send them a copy of both sides of the canceled check

d. wait to see if they will really shut off his phone

In small groups, discuss the answer to the question. If you have a canceled check, bring it to class. When was it cashed? Who cashed it?

COMPARISON SHOPPING

Read these ads for notebooks. With a partner, decide which is the best buy and why.

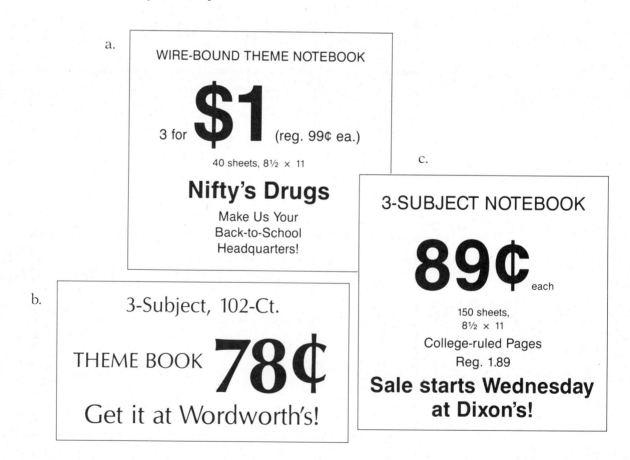

a.
WIRE-BOUND THEME NOTEBOOK

3 for **$1** (reg. 99¢ ea.)

40 sheets, 8½ × 11

Nifty's Drugs

Make Us Your
Back-to-School
Headquarters!

c.
3-SUBJECT NOTEBOOK

89¢ each

150 sheets,
8½ × 11
College-ruled Pages
Reg. 1.89

**Sale starts Wednesday
at Dixon's!**

b.
3-Subject, 102-Ct.

THEME BOOK **78¢**

Get it at Wordworth's!

OPEN-ENDED ACTIVITIES

Choose one or more of the following activities to do outside of class. When you finish, tell the class what you've learned.

1. Go to three different neighborhood banks and compare their service charges, interest rates, the number of people waiting in line, the minimum balance requirements, etc.

2. Design a budget for yourself . . . and try to stick to it.

3. With your classmates, order a subscription to *Consumer Reports*, a nonprofit magazine that protects the consumer by researching and giving information about products (their reliability, safety, and quality). A year's subscription costs around $18.

   Consumer Reports
   Subscription Department
   Box 53029
   Boulder, CO 80321

4. Use a *Consumer Reports* at your local library. Choose an item that interests you (for example, televisions or cars) and compare the brand names listed. Decide which one you would buy.

5. Look in your phone book under "Consumer Complaints" or "Consumer Protection." Call one or more of the organizations and ask what services they provide. If you can't find a list of organizations, call your city councilperson and ask who you should contact if you have a complaint.

6. Apply for a credit card. You can get the applications at banks, department stores, gas stations, etc.

CHAPTER 7

Finding a Place to Live

Look at these pictures. Think (in English) about what you see. Study the words and talk about the scenes.

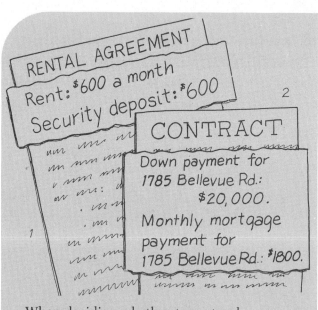

When deciding whether to rent or buy housing, you must consider:
1. the move-in costs (rent and security or cleaning deposit)
2. the down payment and the mortgage payment

You should read these documents carefully:
3. a lease (between a tenant and landlord, usually for a time of six months to a year)
4. a month-to-month rental agreement
5. an insurance policy

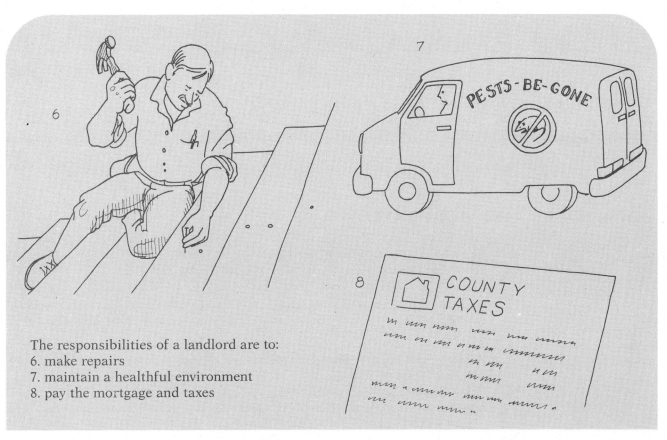

The responsibilities of a landlord are to:
6. make repairs
7. maintain a healthful environment
8. pay the mortgage and taxes

The responsibilities of a tenant are to:
9. keep the property clean
10. not disturb the neighbors
11. pay the rent on time

Renting or Buying

PART A: HOUSING AND YOUR FINANCES

Read this passage to yourself quickly. Don't worry if you don't know all of the words. Just try to understand them in context.

Everyone needs a safe, quiet place to live, shelter from the outside world. But it's not easy to find the right place in the right neighborhood for the right price. First you must consider your finances. If you decide to rent an apartment, in addition to your monthly rent you will probably have to pay move-in costs—the first and last months' rent, a security deposit, and often a cleaning deposit, too. A security deposit is an amount of money the landlord keeps until you move out; the landlord returns the money to you if you leave the apartment in good condition. If you want to buy a house or a condominium, you must consider the down payment (a percentage of the total cost of the house that you pay immediately), your monthly mortgage payment, and the real estate taxes and insurance. Then you must decide how many bedrooms and bathrooms you need and what neighborhood fits your tastes and budget. After you decide these important matters, you can look in the classified ads for housing, drive around the areas that you like, pay a fee to a rental agency, or choose a real-estate agent to find you an apartment or house to rent or buy. Normally, the seller pays the real estate agent's commission.

When apartment or house hunting, it's a good idea to "shop around" to compare values. When you finally find a place you like, be sure to check it carefully: turn on the water faucets, flush the toilets, and check the electricity. Ask if carpets, drapes, refrigerator, stove, etc., are included in the price. Visit the apartment or house during both the day and night to observe the neighborhood.

When you make your final decision, read your rental contract or sales agreement very carefully. It might be a good idea to have a friend look at it too before you sign it.

True or False?

Answer *true* or *false*; then correct the false statements. Read aloud the sentences in the passage that led you to your answers.

1. Real-estate agents help only people who are looking for a house to buy.

2. Before you decide on a house or apartment, you should check the plumbing, electricity, neighborhood, etc.

3. If you like a house or apartment, you should sign a contract right away so that someone else doesn't get it before you do.

4. The only way to find a place to live is to pay an agency to look for one for you.

Vocabulary

Guess the meanings of the underlined words from the contexts. Then match them with the definitions that follow. Write the letters of the definitions in the parentheses.

1. When the loan officer told the Garcías that their monthly mortgage (___) payment would be more than 25 percent of their combined monthly income, they decided they couldn't afford to buy the condominium (___).

2. When the rain started, Cassandra rushed for shelter (___) inside a building.

3. The security deposit (___) on the expensively furnished apartment was $1,000, but the Satos thought they would get all the money back when they moved out.

4. Susan Barnes made commissions (___) of $100,000 in her first year as a real-estate agent (___) because she was honest, energetic, and knew exactly what her clients wanted.

5. When Eduardo Paustnikoff borrowed $10,000 from his friends for the down payment (___) on his dream house, his parents were upset. The cost of the house was beyond his finances (___), and within a year he had lost both the house and his friends!

Definitions

a. an enclosed space that offers protection

b. a percentage of the full price of a house that the buyer pays the seller immediately

c. an agreement between a property owner and someone who buys the property; the property belongs to the lender until the buyer repays all of the money

d. monetary resources

e. a person who acts as a representative for a buyer or seller of land or buildings

f. payment for handling the sale of something—in real estate usually 6 percent of the sales price

g. an amount of money a renter pays in advance for an apartment to pay for any damages; if there is no damage, the landlord returns it when the tenant moves out

h. like an apartment, but the living space is owned, not rented

PART B: HOUSING AND YOUR RIGHTS

Read this passage to yourself quickly. Try to understand new words in context.

Although local laws vary, landlords and tenants have similar responsibilities and rights throughout the United States and Canada. Basically, a landlord must guarantee the tenant a safe and healthy place to live. Plumbing, heaters, electrical wiring, windows, roofs, and locks must be in good condition. The tenant must promise to pay the rent on time, to keep the property clean, and not to disturb the neighbors. Your local rental or consumer office can tell you your specific rights.

If you plan to stay in a place for more than a year, it may be a good idea to sign a lease. A lease is a contract guaranteeing that the landlord will not evict you without good cause or raise the rent, and that you, the tenant, will not move out. If you are not sure of your plans, it's best to sign a month-to-month rental agreement. You aren't as secure, but you won't have to pay a penalty if you decide to move.

When you decide to move—or if your landlord wants to evict you—there must be 30 days' written notice. This will give you time to find a new place to live, and it gives the landlord time to find a new tenant.

Tenants and landlords can often avoid problems if both parties are aware of their responsibilities and if they put all agreements in writing. For example, you may always want to pay your rent by check so that you can prove that the landlord received the money, or you should ask for a receipt if you pay cash.

True or False?

Answer *true* or *false*; then correct the false statements. Read aloud the sentences in the passage that led you to your answers.

1. Any landlord can make a tenant move out *immediately* for any reason.

2. Tenants don't have to pay rent if there is no agreement in writing, so it's a good idea to avoid all contracts.

3. In North America, it is the landlord's responsibility to make repairs (such as plumbing, electricity, etc.) on rental property.

4. A lease guarantees the tenants' right to stay in an apartment for a specific rent and for a specific time, but a month-to-month rental agreement doesn't.

Vocabulary

Guess the meanings of the underlined words from the contexts. Then match them with the definitions that follow. Write the letters of the definitions in the parentheses.

1. Because the tenant (___) in Apartment 231 was so noisy, the manager had to evict (___) him.

2. "I'm sorry I'm late for dinner, dear," he said. "I was discussing the parking garage with the landlord (___)."

3. After they bought the house, the Zavalas installed a water heater with a 10-year guarantee (___).

4. As a penalty (___) for breaking their lease (___), the Dovers lost their last month's rent and the security deposit, but they had no choice when Mr. Dover's company transferred him to another city.

Definitions

a. a person who owns a house or apartment and rents it to others

b. a promise of quality; an agreement to replace, repair, or pay for something if it doesn't work

c. to legally force a tenant to move out of an apartment or house

d. one who pays rent for the use of a room, apartment, or house

e. a punishment—usually financial—for breaking a rule or agreement

f. a written agreement guaranteeing the rent of an apartment or house for a specific length of time

Discussion Questions

Discuss these questions with your classmates.

1. If you could afford either, would you rather rent an apartment or own a house or a condominium? Give reasons for your choice.

2. Have you ever had problems with a landlord or a manager? Describe them.

3. Have you ever had a problem with neighbors? Describe the problem and what you did about it.

4. Have you ever had problems with your plumbing or electricity? Describe what you did.

5. Describe the ideal house or apartment (for you). Consider size, cost, and the neighborhood.

Finding a Place to Live . . . and Staying There

SITUATIONS

Discuss these situations with your classmates. Choose the best answer, in your opinion. (There may not be any one correct answer.) Then compare your answers with the cultural notes that follow.

1. Kasue and Hiroshi Nagaya moved into an apartment. Within a short time, there were cockroaches all over the kitchen and Kasue saw a rat. There was also a hole in the ceiling from a leak in the apartment upstairs. They asked the manager to call an exterminator, a plumber, and a painter, but he refused. They should:
   a. try to get rid of the pests and fix the leak and hole themselves
   b. hire people to do these things and deduct the charges from the rent
   c. move

2. Jorge and Roberto Hernández had lived in the same apartment for 3 years. They were very good tenants. Then the owner hired a new manager who didn't like the Hernández brothers because they were from Mexico. He gave them 30 days' notice to move. They should:
   a. find another apartment
   b. wait for the court notice and then go to court to tell their side of the story
   c. hire a lawyer

3. Sid and Bess Schenkier had been looking for an apartment in Chicago for weeks. The only apartments available cost over $750 a month with 2 months' rent due in advance, plus a $350 security deposit, as move-in costs. Bess found a small, old house outside the city selling for $50,000 with a 10 percent down payment. Their monthly mortgage payments would be $381 a month for 30 years. The best financial solution for them would be:
   a. to rent a nice apartment in the city
   b. to buy the house
   c. to keep looking for a cheaper apartment

4. Gloria Meléndrez has lived in the same apartment for years in a

114

city with rent control (a city in which landlords by law can raise rents only a small percentage each year—for example, 4 percent). The new owner of her building has just raised her rent 15 percent, explaining that Gloria is still paying less than if she had a new apartment. If she complains, he will evict her. She should:
a. pay the new rent
b. find another apartment
c. discuss the problem with the city rent control board

CULTURAL NOTES

1a. It is the responsibility of the landlord to give the tenant a healthy and safe place to live. Cockroaches and rats carry diseases, and holes in walls and ceilings are unsafe. Kasue and Hiroshi shouldn't solve the problems themselves; by doing so they are adding value to the landlord's property at their own expense.

1b. Kasue and Hiroshi should write a letter to the landlord informing him of the problems and giving him a reasonable time in which to solve them. They must also inform him, in writing, that they plan to make repairs and deduct the cost from their rent. (However, the cost of the repairs must not be more than the total month's rent.) Of course, local laws are not all the same, so the Nagayas should first check with the local tenants' organizations to learn about their rights.

1c. Landlords and tenants can usually work out their problems, especially when both understand the law. If the landlord continues to be difficult, the Nagayas might prefer to look for a more pleasant and safer place to live.

2a. They might feel more comfortable in another apartment, but . . . (see 2b).

2b. It is absolutely against the law to discriminate against people because of their race, religion, age, or national origin. Since the Hernández brothers were quiet and clean tenants who always paid their rent on time, they should appeal the eviction notice by appearing in court on the assigned date to explain their side. It would help to bring their canceled checks to prove they had paid their rent on time and statements from neighbors to prove they were quiet and clean.

2c. Hiring a lawyer can be very expensive and they might not need one. They should first check with their local legal aid society or housing authority to see what these agencies recommend.

3a. When you rent, you have no repair responsibilities, you don't have to pay property taxes, and you have few worries. However, you can never be sure when you might have to move out and when the rent might go up. In addition, if you have a fairly good household income, buying a house can be an excellent investment.

3b. If they can pay the down payment of $5,000, they will be saving money each month. The mortgage payment will be less than the rent! They will be investing their money in their future. Because interest payments are tax deductible, they will also save money on taxes. However, the Schenkiers will be totally responsible for the property tax, all repairs, maintenance, gardening, etc. If they don't want that responsibility they should . . . (see 3c).

3c. . . . keep looking for an apartment, or even advertise for an apartment themselves.

4a. Because she lives in a city with rent control, Gloria doesn't *have* to pay the higher rent, but . . . (see 4b).

4b. Her landlord is breaking the law, and she will have to take some action against him if she wants to stay where she is. If she doesn't want to bother, she will have to move.

4c. If she is happy with the apartment, she shouldn't have to move. Since her apartment is under rent control law and her landlord is breaking the law, she should call the rent control board and they will help her.

Buying or Renting

TALKING TO REAL-ESTATE AGENTS

After you find the apartment or house of your dreams in the classified ads or by driving around a neighborhood you like, you usually have to contact a real-estate agent to get the hard facts.

Practice this conversation in pairs:

AGENT:	Thank you for calling Casa Realty. Hi. How can I help you?
CLIENT:	We were driving down High Street and saw your "For Sale" sign at 1785. I saw your ad for a two-bedroom house on Bellevue in the *Times*. My friend told me you knew of some apartments for rent.
AGENT:	Yes, they're asking $94,500 for that little gem, with 20 percent down. Oh, that cozy house rents for just $750 a month, with first and last months' rent plus a $500 refundable security deposit. We have apartments in all price ranges and neighborhoods. Just tell me what you need.
CLIENT:	Oh! That's a little more than I can pay. Do you have any other houses like that for around $50,000 in that neighborhood? That sounds O.K. Are the utilities, stove, and refrigerator included? We need a two-bedroom, furnished apartment for no more than $550 a month, in the Evans Estates neighborhood.

Role-play

Read the following "Residential Rental" ads and the explanation of housing abbreviations. With a partner choose one of the ads and role-play a conversation about it. (Use the preceding conversation as an example.) One of you is the agent, and the other is the client. Then choose another ad and change roles.

RESIDENTIAL RENTALS

2-bd. furn. apt. No lse. Util. pd. $500. 555-8100

3-bdrm., 2-ba. house. New appl., cpt. $1000. 555-2198

Studio for sgl. person. Stv., frig. $450. 555-8910

1 br. condo, gd. vu, sec. bldg. $600. downtown. 555-5687

Large, 4-bd., 2-ba. house, unf. Nice gdn., frpl. $1500. 555-3200

3-bd. apt., new cpts. and drapes, laundry, prkg. $1100. 555-1265

Abbreviations

appl. = appliances
ba. = bathroom
bd., br., bdrm. = bedroom
cpt. = carpet
condo = condominium
frig. = refrigerator
frpl. = fireplace
furn. = furnished
gd. = good
gdn. = garden
lse. = lease
pd. = paid
prkg. = parking
sec. bldg. = security building (has a guard or good system of locks)
sgl. = single
stv. = stove
unf. = unfurnished
util. = utilities (water, gas, electricity)
vu = view

TALKING TO LANDLORDS OR MANAGERS

If you're going to rent an apartment or house, there are a lot of questions you will want to ask the apartment manager or landlord. Make sure you understand *everything* before signing a lease! Practice this conversation in pairs:

APPLICANT: Hi. I just saw your "For Rent" sign. Is the

| three-bedroom apartment |
| house | still available?
| furnished studio |

MANAGER: Yes, it is. Would you like to see it?

| carpeting and drapes |
APPLICANT: Are | a stove and refrigerator | included?
| utilities |

| carpeting |
MANAGER: We furnish | stoves | and pay for the
| air conditioning |

| water. |
| trash pickup. | Parking is ten dollars extra
| gardener. |

| a pool. |
| cable television. |
per month. There is | a laundry room. |
| a parking garage. |
| a recreation room. |

| pets. |
We don't allow | children. |
| subletting.* |

Role-play

Look for real housing ads in your local newspaper. Bring several to class that have a lot of information on what is *included* (for example, utilities) and what is *not allowed* (for example, pets). Working with a partner, take turns role-playing being manager and applicant. Ask and answer questions about the apartments in the ads. Use the preceding conversation as an example.

---

*__subletting__ = *when a renter (not the owner) rents out a house or apartment to someone else, usually for a short time*

Bits and Pieces

TENANTS' RIGHTS

Read this article and discuss it with your classmates. Are your living conditions comfortable, or do you have a landlady like Cecilia Doverkoff? Do you think the punishment she received was fair? Why? Why not?

> ## Slum Lord Jailed (in Own Slum!!)
>
> Cecilia Doverkoff was found guilty yesterday of 15 counts of negligence, endangering the lives of others, and retaliatory eviction. In a landmark sentence, Judge Ronald Kooten sentenced Doverkoff to live 3 months in her own apartment rentals—the Carroll Arms—without the right to leave. "Rat and cockroach infestation, inadequate plumbing, and faulty wiring were just the beginning," said Romelia Sánchez, mother of four and tenant of 14 years. Mrs. Sánchez was served with eviction papers after complaining to the health department. She then took her case to the Legal Aid Society.

FILLING OUT RENTAL APPLICATIONS

Following is the kind of form you have to fill out when a landlord is considering renting an apartment to you. You have to give information about your financial situation and current living situation so the landlord can decide if you would be a reliable person to rent to. Fill in the form with information about yourself.

RENTAL APPLICATION

Name: _____ Age: _____

Spouse's name: _____ Age: _____

Present address: _____
                                   street   city   phone

Present landlord or manager: _____

_____
                                        address   phone

How long at this address? _____ Rent: $_____

Previous address: _____
                                                       street   city

Previous landlord or manager: _____

_____
                                        address   phone

Occupation: _____ Employer: _____

Employer's address and phone: _____

_____ How long employed? _____

Social Security No.: _____ Monthly income: _____

Credit references (names, addresses, account numbers, balances, monthly payments): _____

_____

_____

Personal references (names, addresses, phone numbers): _____

_____

_____

_____

Car (make, model, year): _____ License: _____

Your driver's license: _____ Spouse's driver's license: _____

Have you ever been evicted for disorderly conduct or not paying rent? _____

Any pets? _____ What kind? _____

Number of children: _____ Ages: _____

Name of person to live with you other than spouse or children: _____

I declare that the statements above are true and correct, and I authorize verification of these statements.

DATE: _____ SIGNED: _____

UNDERSTANDING RENTAL AGREEMENTS

Read the following rental agreement and answer the questions.

1. Who is the manager or owner of the property?

2. Who is the person who wants to live in the property?

3. What is the address of the property?

4. Does the applicant have to pay a cleaning charge? A pet deposit? A security deposit?

5. How much has the applicant already paid the owner or manager? How much does he have to pay before May 1?

AGREEMENT TO RENT/RECEIPT OF DEPOSIT

April 14, 19xx

RECEIVED OF *John Smith*, the applicant, *400* dollars as a deposit on the premises known as *123 Garden Street #3* for a term of *1 month*, at a rental rate of *425* dollars per month, rental to begin *May 1*, 19xx. Said deposit is to be applied on the rent and will be retained if the balance is not paid on or before *May 1*, 19xx.

Rent:	$425.00
Security deposit:	225.00
Cleaning charge:	
Key deposit:	15.00
Pet deposit:	50.00
Total amount due:	715.00
Less deposit of:	(400.00)
Balance due on move-in:	315.00

Simon Legree and Associates
1865 Stowe Road
Rome, GA 30163

UNDERSTANDING EVICTION NOTICES

Following is an example of a form a landlord might use if he or she wants a tenant to move out. Working with a partner, read the form and provide common synonyms (words that mean the same thing) for the underlined terms.

NOTICE TO QUIT

(State Code of Civil Procedure Section 1161a, Subdivision 4.)

To: *Romelia Sánchez*

TAKE NOTICE that your month-to-month tenancy of (1) <u>the hereinafter described premises</u> is hereby (2) <u>terminated</u> as of the date thirty (30) days after this NOTICE. You are hereby required (3) <u>to quit and surrender possession</u> thereof to (4) <u>the undersigned</u> on or before the date thirty (30) days after the service of this NOTICE.

The premises of which you are required to surrender possession are known as *Apt. 44B, The Carrol Arms* and situated in the city of *San Felipe*, county of *Los Angeles*, designated by the number and street as: *1887 Angelino St.*

DATED this *6th day of September,* 19 *xx*.

Cecilia Doverkoff
Signature

If you need help, here are some possible synonyms for the underlined terms. Put the number of the underlined term next to its synonym.

a. _____ Cecilia Doverkoff

b. _____ ended

c. _____ 1887 Angelino Street

d. _____ move out

Now discuss with your classmates what you would do if you received a notice like this one.

OPEN-ENDED ACTIVITIES

Choose one or more of the following activities to do outside of class. When you finish, tell the class what you've learned.

1. Look at the apartments advertised in the classified ads and go apartment hunting on a weekend. This will help you learn about housing and improve your English.

2. Look at the houses and condominiums for sale in the classified ads and go to open houses on a weekend. You will get a chance to go inside Americans' houses and to learn about real-estate values and neighborhoods.

3. Write to your state consumer affairs board and ask for information on tenant/landlord laws. Be sure to enclose a self-addressed stamped envelope.

4. Contact your city consumer affairs board or the city housing board and ask for information on city landlord/tenant laws.

CHAPTER 8

Food and Nutrition

Look at these pictures. Think (in English) about what you see. Study the words and talk about the scenes.

Food poisoning can come from the bacteria in:
1. uncooked meat
2. puffed cans
3. food left in the sun

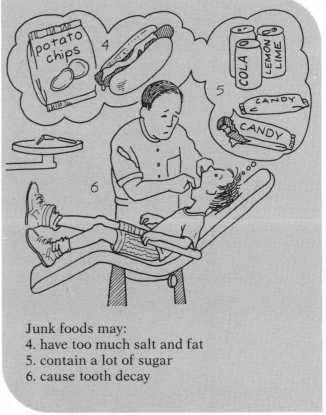

Junk foods may:
4. have too much salt and fat
5. contain a lot of sugar
6. cause tooth decay

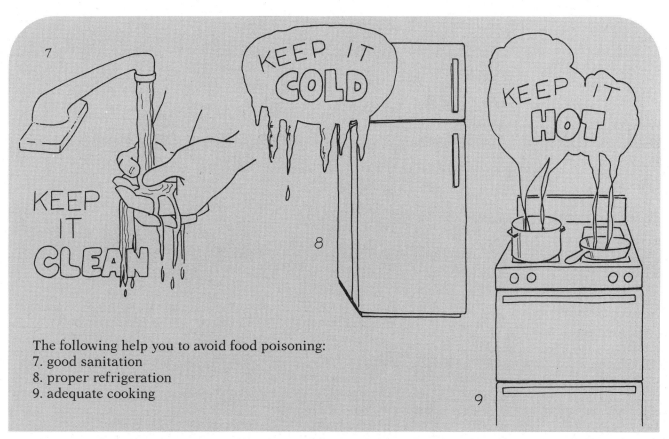

The following help you to avoid food poisoning:
7. good sanitation
8. proper refrigeration
9. adequate cooking

In a restaurant, you:
10. might want a doggie bag
11. can "go dutch"

Food and Health

PART A: EATING AT HOME

Read this passage to yourself quickly. Don't worry if you don't know all of the words. Just try to understand them in context.

Whether you eat to live or live to eat, food should help keep you well. In our modern world of processed and preserved foods, many nutritionists are suggesting that we can stay healthy with a well-balanced diet of plenty of fresh fruits and vegetables and not too much red meat, salt, or sugar. In fact, eating natural, unprocessed foods that are made from scratch, instead of artificial and junk foods, may not only keep you healthy, but save you money, too.

To stay healthy, you must also be careful to avoid food poisoning, a common, unpleasant, and often dangerous illness that affects one out of every six Americans each year. Food poisoning is often caused by salmonella bacteria in food, especially raw meats and dairy products. Heat usually kills the bacteria, and refrigeration keeps them from growing. So remember to keep hot food hot and cold food cold. Also, be sure to keep your hands and cooking utensils clean so you don't transfer germs to the food while you are preparing it.

If you use canned food, always check the cans for leaks or puffiness. A puffed can could mean botulism, a fatal type of food poisoning that you cannot see or smell. Never taste any food that you suspect has spoiled. Instead, return any damaged cans or spoiled food to the grocery store, and the manager will refund your money. When using processed foods, be sure to read all the labels and check the ingredients and the freshness date before you buy or eat the food.

Eating is one of the joys of life. Being careful about what you put in your mouth can keep it that way.

True or False?

Answer *true* or *false*; then correct the false statements. Read aloud the sentences in the passage that led you to your answers.

1. According to most nutritionists, a diet of red meat and sweets is good for you.

2. If a can is puffy, open it and take a little taste to see if the food is still good.

3. Eating raw meat will keep you healthy.

4. Natural, unprocessed food is cheaper than junk food.

Vocabulary

Guess the meanings of the underlined words from the contexts. Then match them with the definitions that follow. Write the letters of the definitions in the parentheses.

1. The factory recalled 5,000 cans of tuna when a family of four died of botulism (___).

2. When you read the label (___) on a product that looks like fruit juice, you may be surprised that the ingredients (___) are nothing but water, sugar, and artificial (___) color and flavors.

3. Nutritionists (___) often work in hospitals, preparing diets for patients with special food needs.

4. Foods made from scratch (___) may spoil faster than processed foods (___), but they're better for you.

5. People can no longer buy turtles as pets for children because the turtles often carry salmonella (___) bacteria (___) that can cause illness in the children who play with them.

6. The picnic ended unhappily when everyone who had eaten the potato salad became ill from food poisoning (___).

Definitions

a. from the beginning, with all the basic ingredients

b. not natural

c. scientists who study the relationship between food and health

d. commercial foods not in their natural state; they usually contain sugar, salt, or chemicals that keep food from spoiling

e. a fatal form of food poisoning, usually found in food improperly canned or preserved at home

f. small, invisible living things that can cause disease

g. contents; things in a mixture

h. a bacteria that causes food poisoning and is usually found in poultry and raw dairy products; heat kills it

i. an illness of the digestive system with symptoms of fever, chills, nausea, vomiting, and diarrhea from 2 to 20 hours after the consumption of bad food

j. a piece of paper or other material containing information about a product

PART B: EATING OUT

Read this passage to yourself quickly. Try to understand new words in context.

Many Americans enjoy dining in restaurants, from fast food chains like McDonald's to family chains like Howard Johnson's to nicer, more expensive restaurants.

If you want to go to a popular restaurant, you should call in advance for reservations. Tell them your name, the time you will be there, and how many people will be in your party. You might also ask if they have smoking and nonsmoking sections, and, if it is a very elegant restaurant, whether men must wear coats and ties.

After the host or hostess seats you and gives you your menu, you will have some time to decide what you want before the waiter or waitress takes your order. Feel free to ask if he or she has a recommendation.

Be sure that the restaurant is clean and the food is well cooked. You can send back any spoiled or uncooked food and the server will either bring you something else, or—if you have lost your appetite—not charge you.

When you pay the bill, don't forget to leave a tip for the waiter or waitress. Usually you leave 15 percent of the total, but if the service was very bad, you don't have to leave anything. If the service was especially good, it's nice to leave a little more. Americans often go to restaurants together and share the bill; this is called "going dutch" or "dutch treat."

If you can't finish your meal, the waiter or waitress might ask if you want a "doggie bag" (or you can ask for one). A doggie bag is a special bag or box for taking your uneaten food home with you. Then you can eat the leftovers the next day.

Eating in restaurants is often fun. You can try different kinds of food, and—best of all—someone else has to wash the dishes!

True or False?

Answer *true* or *false*; then correct the false statements. Read aloud the sentences in the passage that led you to your answers.

1. It's the custom to tip a waiter or waitress 15 percent of the bill.

2. Americans never take leftovers home from a restaurant.

3. If you find dirt in your food, just push it aside. It's your responsibility to pay for what you order.

4. In North America, it's rude to offer to pay only your portion of the bill.

Vocabulary

Guess the meanings of the underlined words from the contexts. Then match them with the definitions that follow. Write the letters of the definitions in the parentheses.

1. The waiter put Linda's uneaten food in a <u>doggie bag</u> (___). She asked for it because she wanted to eat the <u>leftovers</u> (___) for lunch the next day.

2. Her mother told her that "<u>going dutch</u>" (___) with her boyfriend would be a good idea since they made similar salaries.

3. When Nabil got good service from a waiter or waitress he always left a big <u>tip</u> (___). When the service was very bad, he'd leave a penny to show his displeasure.

4. After you get your <u>menu</u> (___), you shouldn't have to wait too long until the waiter <u>takes your order</u> (___).

5. McDonald's is one of the largest restaurant <u>chains</u> (___) in the world.

Definitions

a. a small amount of money a customer gives to someone who has performed a service

b. uneaten food

c. the custom of each person paying for himself or herself

d. groups of connected businesses having the same main owners, menus, etc.

e. a container to take uneaten food home from a restaurant

f. a list of the foods and prices of a restaurant

g. finds out what kind of food a customer in a restaurant wants

Discussion Questions

Discuss these questions with your classmates.

1. Have you ever had food poisoning? What caused it? What happened?

2. Share a favorite recipe for something you make from scratch.

3. Do you have a favorite restaurant that you eat at often? Describe it.

4. Describe your typical diet. Do you think it's well balanced?

5. In your opinion, what are some of the strangest things that people in America eat? What would an American find strange about the diet of people from your culture?

Food and Restaurants

SITUATIONS

Discuss these situations with your classmates. Choose the best answer, in your opinion. (There may not be any one correct answer.) Then compare your answers with the cultural notes that follow.

1. Jonathan Smith is a cook at a very popular restaurant. Because there are so many customers, he's always in a rush, so he rarely has time to wash his hands after he uses the bathroom. He also uses the same knife to cut the tomatoes and lettuce for salad that he uses to cut the chicken for the stew. What do you think might happen?
   a. The customers will be happy because they don't have to wait for the food. What they don't know won't hurt them.
   b. Some of the customers might get sick and think they have the flu.
   c. Some of the customers might get very sick, and the health department will close the restaurant.

2. Arlette Bazin always makes lunch for her husband Pierre. One August day she prepares a sausage sandwich, and Pierre takes it to work in a brown paper bag. It is a hot day and when Pierre takes out his sandwich at noon it feels warm. But the sandwich smells good and Pierre is very hungry. He should:
   a. eat it since it doesn't smell bad
   b. not eat it but give it to a fellow worker
   c. not take any chances and throw it away

3. Tom Michali decides to take his girlfriend to dinner at the Carroll Street Bistro. Because it's a very popular restaurant, he calls ahead for reservations. The restaurant is dark and romantically lit by candlelight. But as they order, Tom notices a cockroach crawling on the table. In addition, when his *coq au vin* is served, the chicken is still pink. Not only that, his knife and fork have food stuck on them. What should he do?
   a. Keep quiet. It would be embarrassing to make a complaint in such a popular restaurant.
   b. Quietly wipe off the knife and fork with a napkin and eat only the cooked parts of the chicken.

   c. Ask the waiter for new silverware, send the chicken back to be cooked more, and quietly tell the manager about the cockroach.

4. At a supermarket, a woman gives William Heffernan a free sample of a new snack called "Potato Crunchies." They taste good, but when Bill reads the list of ingredients on the label he sees: "salt, corn syrup solids, dehydrated potatoes, one of the following: coconut, cottonseed or hydrogenated soy oil; hydrolyzed vegetable protein, mono- and diglycerides, dextrose, propylene glycol mono-esters, sorbitan monostearate, artificial colors and flavors, and butylated hydroxtoluene." He should:
    a. buy three bags because they taste so good
    b. buy one bag to try them out
    c. not eat what he can't pronounce

5. Alice Wu invites Anna Schmidt for lunch in Chinatown. When the bill comes, Anna takes out her wallet so she can pay her share. Alice is insulted when Anna insists on going dutch. Who should pay?
    a. Alice should, because she invited Anna. Alice is right to feel insulted.
    b. Anna should pay her share.
    c. Anna should put away her wallet and invite Alice to lunch in a German restaurant the next week.

CULTURAL NOTES

1a. The customers will be happy at first, but what they don't know might hurt them. Bacteria and germs are invisible and tasteless. Most of the time food that makes us sick tastes exactly the same as good food.

1b. The symptoms of food poisoning can be similar to those of the flu. Although inadequate refrigeration causes 41 percent of food poisoning cases, the unhealthy habits of the people who prepare the food cause 38 percent of these cases. To kill bacteria, cooks should always wash their hands thoroughly with soap and hot water after using the bathroom. Because it's so easy to transfer bacteria from raw meat to foods that won't be cooked, cooks should wash utensils that they have used on raw meat before using them again.

1c. Although some cases of food poisoning are fatal, the customers at Jonathan's restaurant probably won't die. After experiencing fever, chills, vomiting, and diarrhea from 2 to 20 hours after eating the food, however, the customers might feel that they are dying! If many people become ill at the same time, medical investigators might inspect the restaurant. To protect others, they may have to close it.

2a. If Pierre eats the sandwich, he is taking a chance. It may be impossible to tell from the smell if food will make you sick.

2b. If Pierre is unsure whether the sandwich is spoiled, it would be irresponsible to give it to someone else.

2c. Pierre shouldn't risk the unpleasantness and danger of food poisoning. Any food made of meat, eggs, or milk products must be kept either very hot or very cold. Food left in the sun for over 2 hours should be thrown away.

3a. It's embarrassing to complain to strangers, but a little embarrassment is better than getting sick!

3b. If Tom uses the dirty silverware, he risks food poisoning from bacteria. If he eats the uncooked chicken, he runs an even greater risk of poisoning from salmonella bacteria.

3c. Tom must remember that he is paying for the meal, and it's his health he's protecting. He has every right to demand clean utensils and properly prepared food. He should politely tell the manager about the cockroach so that the restaurant can take care of the problem.

4a. The many chemicals that food manufacturers put in processed food may make it taste or look good, but no one knows exactly what effects these chemicals may have.

4b. The chemicals and preservatives in our foods rarely make us sick immediately. But in 20 or 30 years they may cause cancer, heart disease, or dental problems.

4c. If an ingredient is very hard to pronounce, it's probably not a natural food and it may not be good for you.

5a. In Alice's culture, when you invite people to lunch or dinner, you pay for their meals. Alice shouldn't feel insulted, however, because that custom is not part of Anna's culture.

5b. In Anna's culture and in the United States and Canada, many people like to go dutch, each paying a share of the bill. In this way, each person can order what he or she wants and not have to feel uncomfortable about the price.

5c. If Anna realizes that Alice feels uncomfortable with the idea of going dutch, Anna can "pay her back" by taking Alice to lunch another time. She can suggest that, now that they're in America, the third time they might start going dutch. This custom is quite common and applies whether you go out with a friend of the same sex or the opposite sex.

Enjoy Your Meal!

ORDERING IN A RESTAURANT

You often have to make several decisions when eating in a restaurant in the United States or Canada. Take your time when ordering and make sure you get what you want. Don't be afraid to ask questions!

Practice these conversations in pairs:

Conversation 1

WAITER: Hello, here's your menu. Can I bring you anything now?
CUSTOMER: Yes, please. Some water.
WAITER: Here you are. May I take your order?
CUSTOMER: Do you have any recommendations?
WAITER: The pasta with shrimp or crab is very popular. And the salmon is very fresh today.
CUSTOMER: Can you tell me what *fettucini alfredo* is?
WAITER: It's a kind of pasta, with a cream sauce.
CUSTOMER: What's the soup du jour?
WAITER: Today we have cream of mushroom soup.
CUSTOMER: Thanks. I think I need a few more minutes.

Conversation 2

WAITER: Are you ready to order yet?
CUSTOMER: Yes. I'd like the New York pepper steak.
WAITER: Would you like soup or salad?
CUSTOMER: I'd like a salad with the house dressing.
WAITER: Would you like your steak well done, medium, or rare?
CUSTOMER: Medium rare.
   (*After the meal.*)
WAITER: Will there be anything else?
CUSTOMER: Just the check please. Oh, and can I have a doggie bag?
WAITER: Certainly.

Role-play

Read the following menu. With a partner, role-play conversations about it. Take turns being the waiter or waitress and the customer. You might want to know the meaning of the following words:

Béarnaise = a sauce made from butter and egg yolks
du jour = French for "of the day"
filet mignon = a kind of steak, very tender
grilled = cooked over a flame

Dinner

Appetizers

Oyster on the Half Shell	6.00	Clams on the Half Shell	6.00
Prawns Cocktail	6.00	Crab Cocktail	6.00
Steamed Clams (Dozen)	9.50	Steamed Mussels ('Dozen)	9.00

Soups

Soup du Jour	2.50	French Onion Soup	3.50

Salads

Cold Spinach 3.00
House Dressing

Mixed Green Salad 2.00
Vinaigrette or Rocquefort Dressing

Tomato Salad 3.50
With Red Onions, and Vinaigrette Dressing

Duck Salad 9.50
Fresh Spinach, Long Island Duck and Vinaigrette Dressing.

Fresh Pasta Seafood

Curried Pasta with Mussels	9.50	Pasta Primavera	9.00
Pasta with Shrimp	9.95	Green Pasta with Scallops	10.50
Pasta with Crab	9.95	Fettucini Alfredo	8.00

Specialties

Grilled Calf Liver 10.95
With Bacon and Sauteed Onions.

Chicken Saute Sec. 10.50
Herb, Mushrooms, and Wine.

Calf's Sweetbreads 14.50
Sauteed with Mushrooms, and Port Wine.

Pork Chops Prouencale 11.00
Green and Red Peppers, Onions, Garlic and Tomato.

Prime Rib of Beef 12.95
Creamy Horesradish, Baked Potato, and Vegetable.

Roast 'Duck (Half Duck) 13.50
Green Peppercorn Sauce.

house dressing = the special salad dressing of the restaurant
pasta = thin, flour-and-egg noodle-like food
poached = cooked in water or wine
roasted = cooked in an oven
sautée meunière = dipped in flour and cooked quickly in butter
sorbet = a kind of sherbet, or iced dessert

The Promenade Restaurant

From The Ocean
- Fresh Fish -

Seabass with Fine Herbs 13.95
Steamed with White Butter.

Salmon Filet . . . . Market Price
Steamed or Poached, White Butter Sauce and Lemon.

Swordfish 14.50
Grilled or Steamed with Aromatic Herbs.

White Fish 13.95
Saute Meuniere

From the Broiler

Rack of Lamb . . . . 14.95   Filet Mignon Bearnaise 16.50
Roasted with Herbs.

Prime New York Steak . . . . . . 16.50   The Promenade Duet 19.00
Topped with Sauteed Mushrooms.   Petit Filet Mignon with Lobster Tail
                                        and Drawn Butter.

Prime New York Pepper Steak 17.50
Creamy Cognac Sauce.

Above Served with Potatoes of the Day or Rice.

Desserts

Fresh Homemade Pastries and Cakes 3.50
Tarts, Pastries, Cakes Made on the Premises.

Ice Cream and Sorbets 3.00

COMPLAINING ABOUT YOUR ORDER

Remember, you don't have to accept restaurant food that isn't well prepared or conditions that are not sanitary. Just politely tell your waiter or waitress what the problem is, and he or she will correct it. If you have trouble with the waiter, always ask (again, very politely!) to see the manager.

Practice this conversation in pairs:

CUSTOMER: Waiter, | I ordered my steak rare; this is well-done.
this salad has dirt in it.
my glass isn't clean.

WAITER: I'm very sorry. I'll get you another | steak.
salad.
glass.

Would you like to order something else?

CUSTOMER: | No, thank you.
Thank you. I'll have the soup instead.

Role-play

With a partner, role-play conversations in a restaurant. One of you is a waiter or waitress; the other is a customer. Use the menu on pages 134–135 to order. The waiter brings the customer the wrong thing, and the customer complains politely.

CONVERSATION ACTIVITIES

1. Here is an illustration of a table setting in North America:

Compare the drawing with the way you set the table in your culture. Compare how you eat, as well. Where do you place your hands? What kind of utensils do you use? What are some other examples of differences in eating manners in your culture and in North America?

2. Following is a recipe for meatloaf, a traditional American dish. Note: lb. = pound, t = teaspoon, T = tablespoon, C = cup.

Jan's Meatloaf
1 lb ground beef
1 t salt
1 clove crushed garlic
1 T Worcestershire sauce
1 egg
½ C breadcrumbs
½ onion, chopped fine

Mix together all ingredients and put in loaf pan. Bake at 350 degrees for 1 hour.

Discuss your favorite food or a typical dish from your country. You might bring in the recipe and share it with your classmates.

Bits and Pieces

FOOD POISONING

Read these newspaper clippings and discuss them with the class. Has anything like this ever happened to you or someone you know?

Deadly Mushrooms Fell 14 Laotian Refugees

by Irene Clark,
***Globe* Staff Writer**

Seven of fourteen Laotian refugees who ate a deadly species of wild mushrooms appear to be recovering, but 7 have died, Bay Area authorities said Wednesday.

The mushrooms, *Amanita phalloides*, look similar to edible mushrooms in Southeast Asia. A spokeswoman for the Poison Information Center said mushroom poisoning cases occur every year about this time. "The Laotians believe that if they cook the mushrooms with rice and the rice turns red, then the mushrooms are poisonous. This rice didn't turn red," she said, "so they thought it was safe to eat them. Obviously they were wrong."

INDIANA: A.P.

The Indiana Department of Health has recorded 1000 victims of the August 15 GAB Company picnic food poisoning so far. Authorities suspect that the potato salad was the cause, although the boiled ham is still being tested. Marilyn Rosen said, "Luckily, I'm on a diet and just ate the watermelon! We started eating around 11:30, and by 1:00 P.M. a lot of people started running to the bathroom and throwing up. It was just awful." Authorities said that by 4:00 P.M. over 800 picnickers had become ill. The poisoning was probably due to improper refrigeration, a department spokesman said.

MILK ALLERGIES

Do you use dairy products in your country? Does milk give you a stomach ache? Read this article and discuss it.

Gone Sour On Milk?

by Clay Whitehead,
***Times* medical writer**

A study in today's *New England Journal of Medicine* estimated that approximately 80 percent of the world's population is deficient in lactase and cannot digest cow's milk. In the United States, the incidence is much lower—20–25 percent—because of the large number of people of Northern European ancestry.

In Southern Europe, Africa, and Asia, however, milking cows has been a more recent activity—long ago people in these areas did not drink cow's milk. The frequency of the lactase deficiency in these regions is very high, causing individuals to experience an unpleasant gassy, bloated feeling. Calcium requirements are met with diets of soy beans, green vegetables, and seafood.

TABLE MANNERS

Read the following article.

Ask Zenobia

HE EATS LIKE A PIG

by Zenobia Neal

Dear Zenobia,
I've been going with this guy for a year. He's 32 and I'm 29. He's real sweet and works hard and doesn't drink alcohol or chase girls. Maybe I shouldn't complain, Zenobia, but his eating habits make me sick to my stomach. He never waits for me—he starts eating the minute his food is served. He holds his fork in his fist like a child, keeps his left hand on the table, eats real fast, and makes chomping noises. When I try to correct him, he gets angry and says to go eat somewhere else. What should I do? We'll be getting married in 2 months, and I'll die of embarrassment at the wedding dinner.

Sick to My Stomach

Dear Sick,
His refusal to improve his manners proves that he is stubborn and inconsiderate. If you marry this man, you'll be reminded three times each day of the bad choice you made.

Make a list of what Sick to My Stomach's boyfriend does that is considered bad table manners in the United States and Canada. Are all of these considered bad table manners in your culture as well?

UNDERSTANDING FOOD LABELS

By law, most food labels must include a list of the ingredients with the main ingredient listed first, the second next, and so forth. Look at the following labels and fill in the forms. Then, with your classmates, discuss what you have learned. (Note: the words *syrup, dextrose, fructose, honey, corn syrup solids, cereal malt syrup, brown sugar,* and *date sugar* all mean *SUGAR*).

Name of product: _____

How much does the product weigh? _____

Who made the product? _____

From the name on the label, what kind of food do you expect to eat?

_____

What is the first ingredient listed on the label? _____

Name of product: _____

How much does the product weigh? _____

Who made the product? _____

From the name on the label, what kind of food do you expect to eat?

_____

What is the first ingredient listed on the label? _____

141

Name of product: _____

How much does the product weigh? _____

Who made the product? _____

From the name on the label, what kind of food do you expect to eat?

_____

What is the first ingredient listed on the label? _____

OPEN-ENDED ACTIVITIES

Choose one or more of the following activities to do outside of class. When you finish, tell the class what you've learned.

1. Write a letter to the U.S. Department of Agriculture requesting free copies of their food safety publications.

    The publications are:

    Food Safety for the Family FSIS—33
    Summertime Food Safety FSIS—38
    Safe Brown Bag Lunches FSIS—37
    How to Fight the Food Spoilers (mini-poster) FSIS—1255
    Holiday Food Safety FSIS—8

    The address is:

    FSIS Information
    U.S. Department of Agriculture
    Room 1163 S. Building
    14th and Independence Avenue, S.W.
    Washington, DC 20250

2. Write a letter to the U.S. Food and Drug Administration requesting free copies of their current pamphlets on food safety.

    The address is:

    Office of Consumer Affairs
    Food and Drug Administration
    5600 Fishers Lane
    Rockville, MD 20857

3. Write to the Center for Science in the Public Interest and ask for a catalog of their posters and books.

    The address is:

    C.S.P.I.
    1501 16th St., N.W.
    Washington, DC 20036

4. Eat a meal in a restaurant with some of your classmates. Try a restaurant that serves a kind of food that you have never eaten before. Be sure to "go dutch." If you like the food, ask to take your leftovers home.

CHAPTER **9**

In Sickness and Health

Look at these pictures. Think (in English) about what you see. Study the words and talk about the scenes.

When you feel ill, you may need to:
1. describe your symptoms
2. have a prescription filled

Advice for staying healthy:
3. Exercise.
4. Eat fresh food.
5. Don't smoke or eat junk food.

There are special doctors for special needs:
6. A pregnant woman needs an obstetrician.
7. A person with allergies needs an allergist.
8. Children need a pediatrician.

Plan ahead for health emergencies by:
 9. getting immunizations
10. finding a good doctor before you're sick
11. getting insurance before you need it

Staying Healthy

PART A: FINDING A DOCTOR

Read this passage to yourself quickly. Don't worry if you don't know all of the words. Just try to understand them in context.

Getting sick is no fun, especially when you're in a foreign culture. You are far away from your family doctor, and it's often hard to describe your symptoms in English. When you move to a new place, it's a good idea to choose a general practitioner or internist before you get sick. In addition, most people should have a physical checkup every year. Don't feel afraid to "shop around" for a doctor. You can call your local medical association or ask friends and neighbors to recommend someone. Talk with the doctor to see if you feel comfortable with him or her. Be sure the doctor is qualified, that the fees are reasonable, and that you don't have to wait too long in the waiting room.

Besides a general practitioner, many people need one of these specialists as well: a pediatrician for children, a gynecologist for women, an obstetrician for pregnancy, a dermatologist for skin problems, or a psychiatrist for emotional problems. If you have a lot of pain because of strained muscles, you might want to find a good physical therapist, acupuncturist, or chiropractor. Find these specialists *before* you need them!

In the United States, hospital emergency rooms are for serious emergencies. Using the emergency room can be very expensive, so unless you really have an emergency, it's better to call your own doctor to take care of you.

True or False?

Answer *true* or *false*; then correct the false statements. Read aloud the sentences in the passage that led you to your answers.

1. It's considered rude to "shop around" for a doctor; they are all the same.

2. A woman who is expecting a baby should go to an obstetrician.

3. A person with skin problems should see a psychiatrist.

4. If you have the stomach flu or a bad cold, go to a hospital emergency room.

Vocabulary

Guess the meanings of the underlined words from the contexts. Then match them with the definitions that follow. Write the letters of the definitions in the parentheses.

1. He had all the symptoms (___) of appendicitis: a fever, a stomach ache, and a pain in his lower right side, so he immediately called his doctor.

2. It's getting harder and harder to find a general practitioner (___) (G.P.) because most doctors specialize in specific fields of medicine. The closest are internists (___), who can treat most common problems like colds and flu or recommend a specialist to their patients.

3. Going to your doctor when you are well for a yearly checkup (___) often helps stop a medical problem before it gets serious.

4. Mrs. Flores's three-year-old son was having trouble breathing, so she called the pediatrician (___).

Definitions

a. a doctor who specializes in the treatment of diseases of children

b. a doctor who treats all diseases and all parts of the body of men, women, and children; a family doctor

c. the signs that tell you what disease you have

d. a physical examination of your heart, lungs, blood pressure, and general health

e. medical doctors who deal with diseases of the internal organs

PART B: ILLNESSES

Read this passage to yourself quickly. Try to understand new words in context.

Most of us have been ill at least once in our lives, if only because of common childhood diseases such as chicken pox, mumps, or measles; ear infections; sore throats and colds; and stomach flu. We've all probably had a fever (a temperature over 99° Fahrenheit—98.6° is normal) and chills. Some of us have had problems falling asleep because of insomnia, and some of us get tension headaches. Many people have had operations to remove diseased parts of their bodies. Probably everyone has been nauseated and thrown up and had diarrhea at some point in their lives.

Yes, being sick is not a pleasant experience, and we should try to stay as healthy as we can. Some diseases can't be prevented, but if we are careful to get all our immunization shots, watch what we eat, exercise regularly, avoid smoking, and drink alcohol only in moderation, we will probably have a healthy life.

True or False?

Answer *true* or *false*; then correct the false statements. Read aloud the sentences in the passage that led you to your answers.

1. In the United States temperatures are measured in centigrade.

2. Normal body temperature in Fahrenheit is 98.6°.

3. People who are healthy are just lucky; there's really nothing you can do to prevent illness.

4. It is unusual for children to get chicken pox and colds.

Vocabulary

Guess the meanings of the underlined words from the contexts. Then match them with the definitions that follow. Write the letters of the definitions in the parentheses.

1. Living in a war-torn country filled her life with tension (___), and she was very tired because of her insomnia (___).

2. He didn't know whether he had stomach flu or food poisoning. All he knew was that he had a fever (___) of 101°, then he was freezing with chills (___). He had thrown up (___) twice and now he had diarrhea (___). He knew he wouldn't die, but he almost wished he would!

148

3. The doctor gave the young woman an <u>immunization</u> (___) against <u>measles</u> (___) so that she wouldn't get the disease when she got pregnant.

4. The poor Vásquez twins got <u>mumps</u> (___) and <u>chicken pox</u> (___) at the same time. With their swollen jaws and itchy spots, they were miserable.

5. She used to get so seasick whenever she went on a boat that even movies with boats made her <u>nauseated</u> (___).

Definitions

a. when certain substances are put into the body with a needle to make the person safe from a disease

b. emotional pressure causing nervousness

c. an infectious disease with fever and small watery blisters that itch, dry, and may leave scars

d. any temperature of 99°F or more

e. a feeling of coldness or shaking of the body

f. vomited the contents of the stomach through the mouth

g. an infectious disease that causes fever and red spots on the face and body; it can also cause birth defects if a woman has it during pregnancy

h. an infectious disease in which the glands in the neck swell

i. frequent and watery bowel movements

j. sick at one's stomach

k. an inability to sleep at night

Discussion Questions

Discuss these questions with your classmates.

1. What are doctors like in your country? Are general practitioners common? Do they make house calls? Is traditional medicine (acupuncture, the use of herbal remedies, etc.) widely practiced and accepted?

2. Have you ever been extremely ill or had surgery? Describe your experiences.

3. What childhood diseases have you had? Describe them.

4. What immunizations have you had?

Seeking Medical Advice

SITUATIONS

Discuss these situations with your classmates. Choose the best answer, in your opinion. (There may not be any one correct answer.) Then compare your answers with the cultural notes that follow.

1. Grace Yee was sent home from her second-grade class with a bad headache and a skin rash. When Mrs. Yee took her daughter's temperature, the thermometer showed 104°. The mother should:
   a. give Grace some aspirin to lower the fever and get rid of the headache
   b. call the pediatrician
   c. keep Grace warm in bed with a lot of blankets

2. Natasha Pautovsky has had bad headaches ever since she was 12. As she gets older, her headaches are much worse: they are so painful that they make her throw up and they last several days. She should:
   a. borrow her friend Anastasia's prescription painkiller
   b. see a doctor, chiropractor, or acupuncturist
   c. learn to live with the headaches

3. Felipe Ramos is 50 pounds overweight. He is short of breath and has high blood pressure. His only exercise is walking to his refrigerator. The doctor says he has to stop smoking, lose weight, stop eating junk food, and start exercising. He should:
   a. change doctors immediately
   b. not worry because his parents lived until they were 90 and, besides, he feels fine
   c. follow the doctor's advice

4. When Safar Akaba went for his yearly checkup, the doctor told him he needed an operation. Safar didn't feel sick and didn't understand why he needed the surgery. He should:
   a. have the operation because the doctor knows best
   b. ignore the problem because he doesn't feel sick
   c. go to another doctor for a second opinion

5. When Lan Truong went to a new doctor, she had to wait 2 hours in the waiting room. The doctor was impatient with her poor English and her many questions. He hurried through the exam and left as

quickly as possible. When Lan left, the receptionist gave her a bill for $150. She should:

a. pay the bill and continue to see the doctor
b. complain to the doctor about the treatment and the high bill and never go back
c. file a complaint with the medical board

CULTURAL NOTES

1a. Although aspirin helps lower fevers, *never* give it to anyone under 18. If a child's fever is caused by chicken pox or flu, he or she could die because of the aspirin. If you don't know what's causing a fever, there is an aspirin substitute (called *acetaminophen*) available at all drugstores and markets.

1b. It's a good idea to call the doctor immediately and describe the symptoms. The doctor can then decide if they sound serious or not, and what medicines, if any, to prescribe.

1c. By putting blankets on Grace, Mrs. Yee is just raising her temperature. A person with a fever must keep cool and drink plenty of fluids. Blankets are only necessary when the person has chills.

2a. It is very dangerous to take anyone else's prescription medicine, even if you think you have the same symptoms. You must check with your doctor first.

2b. First, Natasha should go to a medical doctor—a neurologist or internist—or a medical headache clinic for a complete physical examination. A doctor can probably tell her what is causing the headaches. He might recommend that she see an allergist or ophthalmologist if he thinks the headaches are caused by allergies or eye problems. She might also try a chiropractor for movement of her neck and spine or an acupuncturist.

2c. If Natasha tries everything in 2b, and still nothing helps, she might have to learn to live with her headaches. She could also try a "pain management" center that tries to teach people to live with chronic pain.

3a. It's human nature to want to ignore unpleasant truths. By changing doctors, Felipe is hoping for more pleasant advice, but he can't change the reality of his bad health, and running away from the truth could be fatal.

3b. The age and health of Felipe's parents won't help Felipe. Even though he doesn't feel sick, he could be. For example, high blood pressure rarely has any symptoms until the person has a heart attack or stroke. Nearly one out of every four adult Americans has high blood pressure!

3c. If Felipe wants to stay alive and healthy, he should stop smoking. There are 350,000 cigarette-related deaths in the United States every year. He should also lose weight and avoid eating too much sugar, salt, or fat. Four thousand Americans die of heart attacks each day. Around 910,000 people will develop cancer each year and one person dies of cancer every 68 seconds! Even though heredity plays an important role, most authorities agree that good health habits, diet, and exercise contribute to the prevention of these diseases.

4a. A doctor is only human and can make mistakes. If you have any doubts or questions about your medical treatment, get another opinion. You must remember that when a doctor recommends surgery, it's on *your* body, *you* will feel the pain, and *you* will pay the bill.

4b. If you take care of a medical problem when it first starts, you may save your life. If you pretend there is no problem, it may get worse.

4c. When you have a serious medical problem, it's a good idea to have a consultation with at least two doctors. Most doctors will recommend that you get a second opinion before you have any serious form of treatment.

5a. Lan should have checked with the doctor's office about the charges before she had her appointment. If she feels the bill is too high, she should discuss it with the receptionist or doctor before paying it. She should continue to see the doctor only if she feels comfortable with him.

5b. Lan should definitely discuss her complaints with the doctor. She must remember that it is *her* body and *her* money, and she has a right to be upset. On the other hand, the doctor might have had an emergency or other problem that day that made him impatient. She could only find this out by discussing her complaints with the doctor.

5c. Not all doctors are good, and if Lan can't work out the problem or receives any treatment she feels is bad, she should call her local medical board and file a complaint.

Seeing the Doctor

MAKING AN APPOINTMENT

When you need to make an appointment with a doctor, write down all of your symptoms (the problems you are concerned about) in English before you call. That way you will feel comfortable with the English words, and you won't forget anything important. If you have Medicare or private insurance, have the information about it with you when you make the call.

Practice this conversation in pairs:

RECEPTIONIST:	Good morning. Doctor's office. Good afternoon. Dr. Whitehead's office.
PATIENT:	Hello. I'd like to make an appointment for

myself	as soon as possible.
my wife	next week.
my son	today.

RECEPTIONIST:	What seems to be the problem? What is the nature of the illness?
PATIENT:	I've been sick since last night. My wife has been feeling ill lately. My son is really sick.
RECEPTIONIST:	Hmmmmm . . . I see . . . Can you describe the symptoms?
PATIENT:	I've been vomiting and nauseated. She thinks she's pregnant. He's got a fever and itchy, red spots on his face and body.
RECEPTIONIST:	Are you a new patient? Have you seen the doctor before?
PATIENT:	Yes. No.
RECEPTIONIST:	Do you have Medicare or other medical insurance?

153

PATIENT: | I have | Blue Cross.
health insurance with my job.
I don't have insurance.

RECEPTIONIST: | Can you come today at 10:00?
The first opening I have is next Tuesday.

TALKING TO THE DOCTOR

Communication is very important during an office visit with a doctor. Make sure you take the list of symptoms you made for the telephone call and a list of any other questions you may have. Don't be afraid to ask what the doctor means if he or she says something you don't understand.

Practice these conversations in groups of four:

Conversation 1

PATIENT: Hi. My name is Eva Deras. I have an appointment for 10:30.
RECEPTIONIST: Yes. Please fill out these forms.
(*A few minutes later.*)
NURSE: Please come this way. Is this your first visit?
PATIENT: Yes.
NURSE: (*after taking the patient's blood pressure, height, and weight*) Here is a gown. Please take off your dress, but you can leave on your underwear.
DOCTOR: (*knocking and entering*) Hello, Miss Deras. What brings you here today?
PATIENT: I just wanted a checkup.
DOCTOR: (*after examining the patient*) Your blood pressure is a little high. And I'd like you to go to the lab for a complete blood count.
PATIENT: When will you get the results?
DOCTOR: I'll call you next week. Meanwhile, I'd say you seem to be in good overall health.

Conversation 2

PATIENT: Hello. I'm Herschel Preisinski. I'm supposed to see the doctor at 2:00.
RECEPTIONIST: Yes. Please have a seat until the nurse calls you.
NURSE: The doctor will see you now.
DOCTOR: Hello, Mr. Preisinski. Now tell me . . . what's bothering you?
PATIENT: I have a bad cough. And I've had chills and a fever since yesterday.
DOCTOR: You should have a chest X-ray.

PATIENT: I just had a chest X-ray a year ago. Frankly, I'd prefer not to have another one at this time.

DOCTOR: Well, I can prescribe a medication for you. You can take two tablets a day and come back in a week if your condition hasn't improved.

Role-play

With a partner, role-play the following conversation by filling in the blanks with the words in the chart that follows. The numbers correspond to the numbers in the conversation. One of you will be the patient, and the other will be the doctor; then change roles.

Conversation

DOCTOR: Hello, _____.
name

What _____
1

_____?

PATIENT: I feel _____. My body _____
2   3

all over. I have _____.
4

Vocabulary

1	2	3	4
are your symptoms	terrible	aches	a temperature
is the problem	awful	hurts	a headache
is the matter	nauseated	itches	a stomach ache
is wrong	weak	is burning	chills and fever
	exhausted	is shaking	diarrhea
	feverish		a rash
			a runny nose
			a bad cough

Bits and Pieces

IMMUNIZATIONS

Read this newspaper article about immunizations against childhood diseases.

Many Diseases a Thing of the Past

ATLANTA:

According to the annual report of the Centers for Disease Control, mumps, measles, diphtheria, whooping cough, and polio have almost disappeared in the United States. This is because of the availability of safe, effective immunizations against these diseases. Moreover, the last occurrence of smallpox was in 1949. Today's children do not need to suffer what their parents and grandparents did before the age of vaccines.

The Centers for Disease Control recommend immunizations for adults as well as children. The CDC also cautions adults—especially those who work with their hands—to be reimmunized for tetanus every 10 years. Free immunizations are available through county health departments.

Have you had the following diseases, or have you been immunized against them? If you are a parent, have your children had the diseases or been immunized?

Illness	Check (if "Yes")		Date of Immunization	
	You	Your children	You	Your children
rubella ("German measles")				
mumps				
polio				
tetanus				
diphtheria				
whooping cough				
smallpox				

UNDERSTANDING HOSPITAL ADMITTANCE FORMS

Read the hospital admittance form on the next page and answer the following questions.

1. Who is the patient? How old is he?

2. What clinic is the patient going to?

3. Who are the patient's parents? Are they married? Divorced? Is the child adopted? "Natural"?

4. Do both the parents work?

5. Do they have insurance? What kind?

BESSIE PLATT GLICKSON MEMORIAL HOSPITAL
PRE-REGISTRATION FORM

Dear Parent:

To help us improve our services, please completely fill out this form before registration. Thank you!

Has this child been here before?   X   YES   ___   NO
If yes, please present patient's I.D. card.

Circle clinic: 1. Hematology/Oncology   4. Dialysis/Transplant

2. Radiation/Oncology   5. Neonatology/Respiratory

(3.) Allergy/Immunology   6. _____

Clinic Physician's Name: Dr. Smith

Was your child referred here by a private physician?   ___ YES   X   NO

Doctor: _____   Phone: _____

PATIENT INFORMATION

Chafian	Richard	8/23/xx	3	M
Last Name	First Name	Birthdate	Age	Sex

504 Elm St.	Miami	FL	33133	555-7731
Address	City	State	Zip Code	Phone Number

FATHER INFORMATION	MOTHER INFORMATION
Robert Chafian	Sue Chafian Wong
Name	Name Maiden
504 Elm St.	504 Elm St.
Address	Address
Miami FL 33133	Miami FL 33133
City State Zip Code	City State Zip Code
555-7731 555-1068	555-7731 555-4500
Home Phone Work Phone	Home Phone Work Phone
Marital Status (circle one): S (M) D W	Marital Status (circle one): S (M) D W
Parental Status (circle one): (Nat'l) Adopt.	Parental Status (circle one): (Nat'l) Adopt.
Foster Step	Foster Step
547-68-0000 M0576909	288-00-9500 TX831257
Social Security # Driver's License #	Social Security # Driver's License #
Barry University	The English Center
Employer's Name	Employer's Name
11300 N.E. 2nd Avenue	3501 S.W. 28th Street
Address	Address
Miami FL 33161	Miami FL 33133
City State Zip Code	City State Zip Code
Green Cross	
Name of Insurance Company	Name of Insurance Company
Billing Address	Billing Address
City State Zip Code	City State Zip Code
39X50112-3 G41091	
Group Insurance # Certificate/Policy #	Group Insurance # Certificate/Policy #

Cat. #46-1432 (Rev. 8/81)   Date: _____

FILLING OUT HEALTH INSURANCE FORMS

In groups, read the following health insurance form. Make sure you understand the vocabulary. (Ask your teacher or use a dictionary if you are unsure of some of the important words.) Then each person in the group should complete the form for himself or herself.

---

1. TYPE OF APPLICATION: PLEASE CHECK THE APPROPRIATE BOX.

☐ NEW ENROLLMENT
01

☐ CHANGE OF COVERAGE
02

☐ ADDING FAMILY MEMBER TO EXISTING BLUE CROSS MEMBERSHIP
03

---

2. CHOICE OF COVERAGE: PLEASE CHECK THE BOX FOR YOUR CHOICE OF COVERAGE.

☐ PERSONAL PRUDENT BUYER $250 DEDUCTIBLE 01

☐ PERSONAL PRUDENT BUYER $500 DEDUCTIBLE 02

☐ PERSONAL PRUDENT BUYER $1000 DEDUCTIBLE 03

☐ PERSONAL PRUDENT BUYER BASIC 04

☐ MAJOR PROTECTION $200 DEDUCTIBLE 05

☐ MAJOR PROTECTION $500 DEDUCTIBLE 06

☐ MAJOR PROTECTION $1000 DEDUCTIBLE 07

☐ BASIC PROTECTION 08

☐ COMMUNICARE 09

INDICATE CLINIC NAME AND PMG #

_____

---

3. APPLICANT INFORMATION

LAST NAME	FIRST NAME	MI	CHECK ONE	SOCIAL SECURITY NO.
			☐ SINGLE ☐ WIDOWED ☐ MARRIED ☐ DIVORCED	

STREET ADDRESS	CITY	STATE	ZIP CODE	HOME PHONE ( )

BILLING ADDRESS IF DIFFERENT FROM ABOVE	CITY	STATE	ZIP CODE	BUSINESS PHONE ( )

OCCUPATION	SPOUSE SOCIAL SECURITY NUMBER	HAS ANYONE ON THIS APPLICATION BEEN A MEMBER WITHIN THE LAST 5 YEARS? ☐ YES ☐ NO	STILL ENROLLED ☐ YES ☐ NO	DATE CANCELLED MO / DAY / YR

NAME OF MEMBER	CERTIFICATE OR ID NO.	GROUP NO.	

---

4. APPLICANT/FAMILY INFORMATION: LIST ALL ELIGIBLE FAMILY MEMBERS TO BE ENROLLED INCLUDING YOURSELF. IF SPOUSE'S LAST NAME IS DIFFERENT FROM YOURS, PLEASE EXPLAIN.

	LAST NAME	FIRST NAME	MI	HEIGHT	WEIGHT	AGE	BIRTHDATE MO / DAY / YEAR	WAIVER 1	WAIVER 1 DATE DURATION	WAIVER 2	WAIVER 2 DATE DURATION
10 ☐ MALE 20 ☐ FEMALE	APPLICANT										
30 ☐ HUSBAND 40 ☐ WIFE	SPOUSE										
50 ☐ SON 70 ☐ DAUGHTER											
51 ☐ SON 71 ☐ DAUGHTER											
52 ☐ SON 72 ☐ DAUGHTER											
53 ☐ SON 73 ☐ DAUGHTER											

Please print.

	(APPLICANT'S NAME)

7. IF YOU WISH TO COVER CHILDREN BETWEEN THE AGES OF 19 TO 23, COMPLETE THE FOLLOWING:

DEPENDENT'S NAME	MARITAL STATUS
	☐ SINGLE ☐ MARRIED
DEPENDENT'S NAME	☐ SINGLE ☐ MARRIED

I claim my son(s)/daughter(s) as a dependent on my Federal Income Tax ☐ Yes ☐ No

8. HEALTH HISTORY OF YOU AND YOUR FAMILY: Include information on all family members you wish to cover.

HAVE YOU OR ANY OF YOUR FAMILY MEMBERS LISTED ON THIS APPLICATION HAD OR EVER BEEN TREATED BY A PHYSICIAN OR ANY HEALTH CARE PROFESSIONAL FOR ANY OF THE FOLLOWING CONDITIONS? ANSWER "YES" OR "NO" FOR EACH CONDITION. IF YOU HAVE EVER HAD OR BEEN TREATED FOR A CONDITION NOT LISTED, PLEASE INDICATE THE CONDITION(S) IN BOXES 60-64.

CONDITION	YES	NO	CONDITION	YES	NO	CONDITION	YES	NO	CONDITION	YES	NO
1. Abnormal Jaw Closure			18. Diarrhea			33. Intestinal/Stomach/ Colon Problems			48. Rheumatic Fever		
2. Alcohol/Drug Abuse			19. Diseases of Eyes (Other than Corrective Lenses)						49. Skin Disorders		
3. Allergies/Hayfever/ Sinus						34. Jaundice			50. Stroke		
						35. Joint Pains/Disorders			51. Surgical Operations		
4. Anemia			20. Disease/Disorders of Ears, Nose, Throat			36. Knee Problems			52. Thyroid Disorders/ Goiter		
5. Arthritis						37. Liver Problems/ Hepatitis					
6. Asthma			21. Dizziness/Fainting Spells						53. Tuberculosis		
7. Attempted Suicide						38. Lung Disease/ Breathing Problems			54. Tumors/Growths/Cysts		
8. Back or Spinal Injuries/Disorders			22. Emphysema						55. Ulcers		
			23. Female Genital/ Reproductive Organ Problems			39. Male Genital Problems			56. Urinary/Kidney/ Bladder Problems		
9. Breast Disorders						40. Mental Disorders					
10. Bronchitis						41. Mental Retardation			57. Varicose Veins		
11. Cancer			24. Foot Problems			42. Nervous/Emotional Disorders			58. Vein/Artery Diseases		
12. Chest Pains			25. Fluid Retention						59. Venereal Disease		
13. Colitis			26. Gallbladder Problems			43. Paralysis			List any other condition not mentioned above.		
14. Convulsive Disorders Seizures/Epilepsy			27. Gout			44. Parkinson's Disease					
			28. Headaches/Migraines			45. Polio			60.		
Diabetes			29. Heart Disease			46. Raynaud's Disease			61.		
15. Insulin Dependent			30. Hernia			47. Rectal Disorders/ Bleeding or Hemorrhoids			62.		
16. Oral Medication			31. Herpes						63.		
17. Diet Only			32. High Blood Pressure						64.		

PLEASE ANSWER "YES" OR "NO" TO THE FOLLOWING QUESTIONS:

65. HAS ANY PERSON ON THIS APPLICATION EVER HAD AN APPLICATION FOR HEALTH INSURANCE DENIED OR RESTRICTED? ☐ YES ☐ NO

66. HAS ANY PERSON ON THIS APPLICATION EVER HAD, APPLIED FOR OR BEEN ELIGIBLE FOR MEDICARE DISABILITY HEALTH INSURANCE PLAN? ☐ YES ☐ NO

67. DOES ANY PERSON ON THIS APPLICATION HAVE ANY SIGNS OR SYMPTOMS FOR WHICH HE/SHE HAS NOT YET CONSULTED A PHYSICIAN, PSYCHOLOGIST OR OTHER HEALTH CARE PROFESSIONAL? ☐ YES ☐ NO

HAS ANY PERSON(S) LISTED ON THIS APPLICATION:

68. BEEN HOSPITALIZED WITHIN THE LAST 5 YEARS? ☐ YES ☐ NO

69. SEEN A PHYSICIAN, PSYCHOLOGIST OR OTHER HEALTH CARE PROFESSIONAL WITHIN THE LAST 5 YEARS? ☐ YES ☐ NO

70. HAD FUTURE MEDICAL, SURGICAL OR PSYCHIATRIC TREATMENT RECOMMENDED WITHIN THE LAST 5 YEARS? ☐ YES ☐ NO

71. EVER HAD SIGNS OR SYMPTOMS OF DRUG OR ALCOHOL ABUSE PROBLEMS OR BEEN ORDERED BY THE COURT TO RECEIVE TREATMENT? ☐ YES ☐ NO

72. EVER HAD PREGNANCY DELIVERED BY CESAREAN SECTION? ☐ YES ☐ NO

73. EVER HAD SURGERY PERFORMED WITHIN THE LAST 5 YEARS? ☐ YES ☐ NO

74. IS ANY PERSON LISTED ON THIS APPLICATION CURRENTLY PREGNANT? ☐ YES ☐ NO

75. DOES ANY PERSON LISTED ON THIS APPLICATION HAVE ANY OTHER CONDITIONS, IMPAIRMENT OR DEFORMITIES NOT DISCLOSED ELSEWHERE ON THIS APPLICATION? ☐ YES ☐ NO

3

OPEN-ENDED ACTIVITIES

Choose one or more of the following activities to do outside of class. When you finish, tell the class what you've learned.

1. If you don't already have a doctor, find one.

2. If you don't already have a dentist, get one.

3. If you don't already have health insurance, find out how much it will cost and what kind is the best for you.

4. Write or call the American Heart Association, the American Cancer Society, and the American Lung Association and ask for their free pamphlets. Then read them! The pamphlets will help your English and your health.

5. If you smoke, stop! Many hospitals and community health organizations have classes to help you stop. Find out about one.

6. If you don't exercise, start! Investigate different community organizations, local parks, the Y.M.C.A., etc. for their exercise classes. It's a nice way to stay healthy and to make American friends.

7. Keep a journal of what you eat, what you do, and how you feel for one month. Be honest with yourself. Then look at it and see if what you eat affects how you feel. You'll be surprised at the results. Be sure to keep the journal in English.

CHAPTER 10

Education in the United States

Look at these pictures. Think (in English) about what you see. Study the words and talk about the scenes.

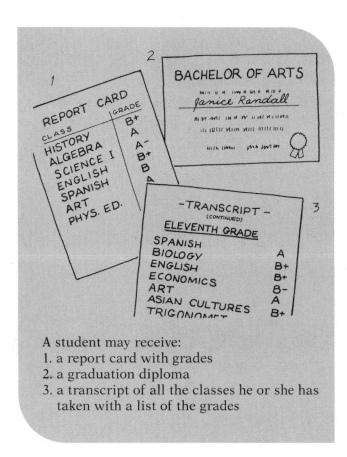

A student may receive:
1. a report card with grades
2. a graduation diploma
3. a transcript of all the classes he or she has taken with a list of the grades

To attend a college or university, you might need to:
4. pay tuition
5. get a scholarship
6. take the TOEFL test

In the United States and Canada, students attend:
7. elementary school
8. junior high school
9. high school

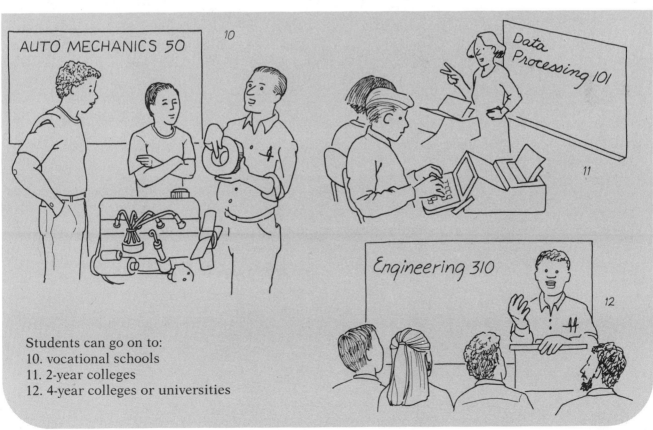

Students can go on to:
10. vocational schools
11. 2-year colleges
12. 4-year colleges or universities

Schools in the United States

PART A: GENERAL EDUCATION

Read this passage to yourself quickly. Don't worry if you don't know all of the words. Just try to understand them in context.

A democracy must have well-educated citizens who are able to think for themselves and make decisions in elections. In the United States, education is free and compulsory for everyone. Although public education is the responsibility of each state, all 50 states have laws that all children must attend school from the time they are 5, 6, or 7 until they are 16, 17, or 18. (The law varies, depending on the state.)

Before the start of mandatory education, children often go to private nursery schools or public preschools. At 5, they usually enter kindergarten at an elementary school. Children then go on to grades 1 to 6, where they learn the basics of reading, writing, arithmetic, history, and geography. After elementary school (also called *grammar school*), children attend junior high for grades 7, 8, and 9. Then they attend high school for grades 10, 11, and 12, where they concentrate on subjects preparing them for college or a job. Some states do not have a junior high school level; in these states, grammar school ends with the eighth grade, and high school begins with the ninth grade.

True or False?

Answer *true* or *false*; then correct the false statements. Read aloud the sentences in the passage that led you to your answers.

1. Free public education is a luxury in a democracy and not a necessity.

2. In the United States, if parents don't want to send their children to school, they don't have to.

3. Every state has junior high schools.

4. The age at which children begin compulsory education in the United States varies from state to state.

Vocabulary

Guess the meanings of the underlined words from the contexts. Then match them with the definitions that follow. Write the letters of the definitions in the parentheses.

1. In most states, children cannot leave school until age 16; education is <u>compulsory</u> (___).

2. When you look at a map and study the <u>geography</u> (___) of a country, you can better understand its history.

3. Many children who failed in <u>grammar school</u> (___) became successful as adults; the inventor Thomas Edison is a good example.

4. Many working parents send their children to <u>nursery school</u> (___).

Definitions

a. preschool classes for children ages 2 to 4½

b. necessary or obligatory by law

c. the first six or eight grades of school, also called *elementary school* or *primary school*

d. study of the countries of the world, seas, rivers, cities, etc.

PART B: HIGHER EDUCATION

Read this passage to yourself quickly. Try to understand new words in context.

In general, "higher education" refers to an educational program a person pursues after high school. There are various types of higher education in the United States. In vocational schools, students can train for a job. In community colleges, they can either train for a job or prepare for further education. Then there are 4-year colleges or universities, where most students are preparing for a profession. Colleges and universities are essentially the same, although a university usually offers more subject areas, grants postgraduate degrees, and may have higher entrance requirements.

Different colleges and universities have different entrance requirements. To attend a 2-year college, you usually just have to be 18 or over. In some cases, you don't even need a high school diploma. Four-year college and university entrance requirements vary; you need a certain minimum grade point average (GPA) on your high school transcripts, and you must achieve certain scores on the college entrance exam for most schools. However, some allow lower averages and test scores than others.

College tuition and fees vary greatly. In the same state, you might find 2-year colleges that are completely free and private universities costing thousands of dollars per semester. Usually, the tuition is much higher for nonresidents than for those who have lived in the state for a year or more. Because of these high costs, scholarships or low-interest student loans are often available to students who meet certain requirements.

True or False?

Answer *true* or *false*; then correct the false statements. Read aloud the sentences in the passage that led you to your answers.

1. You must graduate from high school before you can attend a community college or job training school.

2. Residents of the state usually pay less money to go to their state college than nonresidents do.

3. College entrance requirements are the same throughout the United States.

4. A person wishing vocational training should probably go to a university.

Vocabulary

Guess the meanings of the underlined words from the contexts. Then match them with the definitions that follow. Write the letters of the definitions in the parentheses.

1. College <u>tuition</u> (___) charges can range from $20 to $14,000 per year.

2. In order to get most <u>scholarships</u> (___), you have to have both good grades and financial need.

3. It's a good idea to have several copies of your <u>transcripts</u> (___) and your <u>diploma</u> (___) so you can show them to people when applying for school or a job.

Definitions

a. official paper showing the successful completion of a course of study

b. records of grades, completed courses, teacher's comments, etc.

c. the fee a student pays to attend a school

d. money colleges, universities, or organizations give to students to pay for tuition and other educational costs

Discussion Questions

1. At what age do children usually begin school in your country? At what age do they usually leave?

2. The cost of higher education varies in the United States and Canada. Is this true in your country? Compare the costs in general of attending college in your country and in North America.

3. Are you currently attending a community college, 4-year college, vocational school, or extension program? Compare your higher education program here with one that would have a similar purpose in your country. Think about:

    • entrance requirements

    • length of time required to complete a program

    • tuition and fees

    • level of difficulty of course work

    • the attitudes, behavior, and goals of your fellow students

Taking Tests and Reaching Your Goals

SITUATIONS

Discuss these situations with your classmates. Choose the best answer, in your opinion. (There may not be any one correct answer.) Then compare your answers with the cultural notes that follow.

1. It's time for finals at the University of California, Los Angeles, and Akiko Tetsuya has just learned that her grandmother has died in Tokyo. She is so upset that she can't concentrate on her studies, and she can't sleep at night. In art history, she got a C− on the first midterm exam and an A on the second. If she gets an A on the final, she'll get an A in the class and that will raise her GPA (grade point average). She should:
   a. try to do the best she can on the test
   b. tell the professor about her problems and see if she can take a make-up test later
   c. sit next to the smartest student in the class and copy the answers

2. Jae Don Kim was a builder in Korea. Now, at age 55, he has retired but would like to go back to school to become an architect. His wife and children think he's too old to go back to school. He should:
   a. join some clubs and enjoy his retirement
   b. enroll at the university and study architecture
   c. enroll in classes at a community college for 2 years and then transfer to the university if he enjoys school

3. Pablo Ramírez was a teacher in El Salvador but now lives in the United States. He doesn't approve of the schools in his neighborhood and thinks he can educate his children better at home. He should:
   a. not send his children to school and teach them at home
   b. send them to school but talk with the teachers, explaining his concerns, then work with his children when they do their homework
   c. send them to a private school even though it may cost a lot of money

4. Sue Wong has always been a straight-A student. She studied English for 10 years in her home country and is now in San Francisco on a foreign student visa. She wants to go to the University of California, Berkeley or Stanford University. She takes the TOEFL test. She gets such a low score that she feels terribly ashamed. What should she do?
   a. She should go back to her country because she is a failure.
   b. She should enroll in an intensive English course and, at the same time, practice taking tests from a TOEFL preparation book. Then she should take the test again and again until she gets a good score.
   c. She should go to a community college to improve her English and become accustomed to the American college system. Then, in her junior year, she can transfer to Berkeley or Stanford.

5. Janet Glickson is a grandmother. She has always wanted to learn French. She should:
   a. buy a French book and teach herself
   b. forget about it; it's too hard to learn new things when you are older and have been away from school for many years
   c. take a class in French at her local community college or the local recreation center

CULTURAL NOTES

1a. In the United States and Canada, most teachers understand that students have good days and bad days. Akiko can try to force herself to concentrate and do the best she can—but first she should try the following (see 1b).

1b. Many times teachers understand personal problems and will try to help their students. If you are quite ill or if you have just received distressing news, you can often take a make-up exam at a later date. (It might be harder than the original exam, however.) Also, if you are unhappy or confused about the grade you got, you should talk it over with your teacher. It could have been a mistake that the teacher can correct.

1c. Cheating is unacceptable in the United States and Canada. If you fail a test, you often get a second chance; if you are caught cheating, school officials may ask you to leave the school.

2a. A leisurely retirement is wonderful for some, but Jae Don obviously wants to do more with his free time. Many older people attend college in the United States, some for the very first time in their lives! Jae Don shouldn't be concerned with what others think; it's his life and his happiness and he should try to achieve his goals as best he can.

2b. Since he's been away from school for such a long time, it might not be easy for Jae Don to enroll in the university. The work might be too difficult, the English too hard, and he might get frustrated and quit.

2c. Jae Don should go to a community college and pursue his goal. It should be easy for him to get in, and then he can see if he enjoys his studies. The most important thing for him to remember is that he's never too old to change and grow.

3a. In the United States, school attendance is mandatory for children; in most states, Pablo would be breaking the law if he refused to send his children to school.

3b. Parents often disagree with the techniques of their children's teachers. Pablo has a right to express his concerns to the principal and the teachers. If he really objects to the programs, he can teach his children his point of view at home.

3c. Pablo can look for a school that shares his ideas and send his children there. Private schools are available for those who don't want to send their children to public schools, but they do cost a lot of money. Scholarships are sometimes available to help those who can't afford the tuition.

4a. Sue shouldn't feel ashamed of herself because she got a low score. She should feel proud that she was brave enough to take a very difficult test. Studying English in your country doesn't mean that your English is perfect!

4b. If Sue doesn't do well on the TOEFL exam, it only means that she isn't ready to study in an American university. It would be too difficult for her to understand the lectures, take notes, read all the books, and write all the papers. By taking ESL classes and practicing for the TOEFL test, she will better prepare herself in English.

4c. It wouldn't be easy for Sue to compete with the very best university students in their native language. By going to a community college she will have 2 years to improve her English and study skills and to better prepare for the more difficult university courses.

5a. It's almost impossible to learn a foreign language well by yourself. Besides, it's boring!

5b. You're never too old to learn something new if you're really motivated.

5c. Most cities offer free or inexpensive classes at local parks, night schools, the YMCA, etc. Adults can take classes in photography, cooking, sewing, swimming, art, foreign languages, etc. Many community colleges and universities have an extension program where you can take classes without being a full-time student. You'll be surprised when you see all the different classes offered at your local colleges. And, it's a great way to meet new friends!

SECTION 3

Getting the Most out of Your Education

MAKING APPOINTMENTS WITH INSTRUCTORS

Although your teacher may seem busy, he or she will probably be willing to see you individually outside of class. You may want to discuss an assignment that you don't understand or have a grade clarified. Don't hesitate to make an appointment with your instructor whenever you feel you need extra help.

Practice this conversation in pairs:

STUDENT: | Professor Marks,
 Mr. Green,
 Ms. Jones,

I'd like to make an appointment | to see you.
 with you.

TEACHER: | Sure.
 Certainly.
 O.K. | I have office hours on Wednesday, between two and four.
 I'm free Monday, Wednesday, and Friday mornings before class.
 What time is good for you?

STUDENT: | Can I come this Wednesday, then?
 How is this Monday at nine?
 I work, so I don't have much free time. How about right after class?

TEACHER: | That's fine. Just drop by.
 This Monday at nine? Sorry, I have another appointment then. How about next Monday?
 That's all right for me.

STUDENT: Thank you. | I'll see you then.
 Next Monday is fine.

Role-play

With a partner, role-play a conversation about making an appointment. You are a student, and your partner is a teacher. The first time you suggest is not good for the "teacher," but finally you decide on a time. Then change roles.

ASKING AN INSTRUCTOR FOR HELP

Once you've made your appointment, think about what you are going to say to your instructor. Be direct: North Americans appreciate directness. They usually want to "get down to business" right away.
    Practice this conversation in pairs:

TEACHER: Well,	Nabil, Ms. Sánchez, Anya,	what did you want to see me about? what can I do for you? how can I help you?

STUDENT: Mr./Ms./Professor _____, I was wondering if you

could explain	this grade to me. this paragraph in our reading book. what's wrong with my assignment.

TEACHER:	Certainly. Sure. O.K.	I'd be happy to.

STUDENT:	Thank you. O.K.

I don't understand	why I got a C instead of a B. what these words mean. your correction marks.

Role-play

Work with a partner. One is the student, and the other is the teacher. The student has come to the teacher's office to discuss one of these problems:

- a grade he or she feels should be higher
- a difficult passage in a reading textbook
- a troublesome grammar point
- a word or expression he or she doesn't understand
- a student in the class who is bothering him or her
- a difficult assignment
- (a real problem of your own)

Then change roles.

Bits and Pieces

YOU'RE NEVER TOO OLD TO LEARN!

Read the following article and discuss it in small groups. Do you agree with Clara Vásquez?

Homecoming . . . The Long Way Around

by Yvonne Nishio
Morning Star **reporter**

Students at Eastlake College chose Clara Vásquez to be this year's homecoming queen. Vásquez, with a major in art and a minor in English, got her degree the hard way. It's been 40 years since she first tried to get a college diploma and that was 12 years after she dropped out of high school. Family problems and lack of money made pursuing higher education impossible. Vásquez, a grandmother of five, says age is of no concern to her. "If you want to graduate, there's no excuse not to," she said. "The opportunity is out there. All you have to do is take advantage of it."

CHEATING

Read this news article and discuss it in small groups. How is academic cheating regarded in your country?

Nine in College Cheating Case Suspended

by Harold Preis
Times **staff writer**

Nine university students have been suspended for 1 year and have been barred from participating in any fraternities or sororities on campus after officials ruled that they collaborated to cheat on a final examination last semester.

The students—seven men and two women—were told of the suspension yesterday. The allegations of cheating were first made May 14, after a committee of faculty members determined that the similarities in the nine exams were not coincidental.

TESTS

You are going to take some practice tests. The test questions are based on information you have seen in previous chapters. Be sure to stop before each new section and discuss the different forms, the answers, and the strategies for answering the various types of tests. Be sure to follow the instructions.

The Answer Sheet

Look at the form below. Answer the questions, then fill in your name, the date, etc., on the form.

1. How will this answer sheet be scored?

2. Should you use pen or pencil? Why?

3. If you make a mistake, how do you change your answer? Why?

4. Do you mark the answers with a check (√), circle (○) or bar (━)?

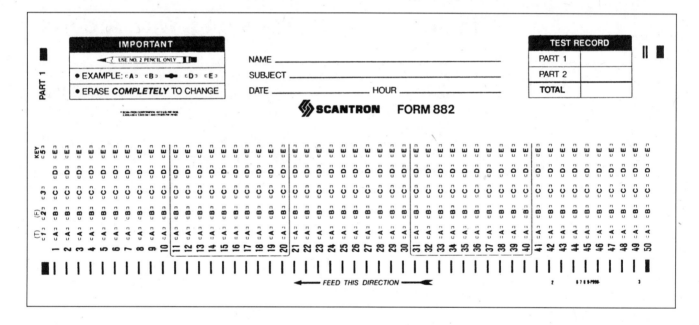

A. True/False Questions

This is the easiest kind of test; you have a 50 percent chance of answering correctly. (You also have a 50 percent chance of making a mistake!) Be sure you understand *every* word before answering, especially the use of negatives.

Answer *true* or *false* by filling in Column T or F on the answer sheet.

1. R.S.V.P. means "really very special person."
2. A paramedic helps in a medical emergency.
3. He "passed away" is not a euphemism.
4. You can't buy traveler's checks unless you have a bank account.
5. The usual tip for a waiter or waitress in the United States is 15 percent of the bill.

NOW STOP . . . do not continue until told to do so.

B. Multiple-Choice Questions

In this test you are given part of a sentence and a choice of ways to finish it. If you studied, the choice of answers will help you. If you didn't study, you can always guess! Be sure to read all the choices before deciding on the right answer.

Complete these sentences by filling in the letter of the correct answer on your answer sheet.

6. When someone invites you to a party in the United States or Canada you should:

    a. come early
    b. come late
    c. come on time

7. A public library can give you information about:

    a. American history
    b. cooking recipes
    c. popular songs
    d. all of the above
    e. none of the above

8. The euphemism for *fat* is:

    a. slim
    b. skinny
    c. lean
    d. all of the above
    e. none of the above

NOW STOP . . . do not continue until told to do so.

C. Matching

This test is easy except there's usually one more answer than question, so it's hard to guess.

Match each item in Column A with the correct phrase from Column B, then fill in the correct letters on the answer sheet.

A. *In the case of:*

9. an earthquake
10. heart attack
11. a downed power line
12. a robbery

B. *you should:*

a. call the police
b. call the gas company
c. call the electric company
d. stand in a doorway
e. call the paramedics or fire department

NOW STOP . . . do not continue until told to do so.

D. Completion

This test gives you a chance to show your knowledge. Often there is more than one right answer.

Take out a clean piece of paper, number from 13 to 16, and write the missing words in these sentences on your paper, not on the answer sheet.

13. The _____ and the landlord sign a lease.
14. People usually send party invitations 3 weeks _____ .
15. Another name for grammar school is _____ .
16. A list of the foods a restaurant has is a _____ .

NOW STOP . . . do not continue until told to do so.

E. Essay

Turn over your paper and write two paragraphs comparing and contrasting education in the United States or Canada and education in your country. Be sure to use as many facts as you can. You have 15 minutes.

Now proceed to Section F.

F. Reading Comprehension

It helps to read the questions first; then you know what answers to look for. Read as quickly as you can, skimming for the answer; you are not reading for enjoyment!

Read this passage and then answer the questions by filling in the correct letters on your answer sheet.

YOU HAVE 5 MINUTES TO COMPLETE THIS SECTION.

Approximately 250,000 students from 170 countries take the TOEFL test each year. This 150-question, 120-minute test has been given to foreign students since 1963 to test their proficiency in English. The test consists of three parts: listening comprehension, reading comprehension, and vocabulary. A machine-scored answer sheet is used, and all questions are multiple choice.

The TOEFL is offered twelve times each year on specific Saturdays in August, October, November, January, March, and May and on six specific Fridays the other months. It is given at designated test centers throughout the United States and Canada, and foreign countries as well.

A student may take the TOEFL as many times as necessary to achieve the score needed, but the student must reregister each time and pay the fee. There are no passing or failing scores on the TOEFL, and different colleges and universities have different admittance scores. Generally, one must get a score of 550 or more to attend an American university; admission to a 2-year college is possible with a score of 449, or sometimes even less.

The TOEFL score is valid for 2 years, and the highest score is the one considered.

There are many practice test booklets for sale that include sample questions from former tests, plus tapes for the listening comprehension section. Experts recommend that students study from these books to prepare for the real exam.

Always pay attention to the question number on your answer sheet. Are you filling in Question 17? You don't have to answer the questions in order. Do the easier ones first, then go back and do the harder ones. When you don't know an answer, guess.

---

17. The TOEFL test is given _____ .
    a. twelve times each year
    b. on specific Saturdays
    c. on specific Fridays
    d. all of the above
    e. none of the above

18. Each year about _____ students take the TOEFL test.
    a. 250,000
    b. 120,000
    c. 135,000
    d. 70,000
    e. 449

19. The TOEFL score is valid _____ .
    a. for 6 months
    b. for 12 months
    c. for 18 months
    d. for 24 months
    e. forever

20. Most universities will admit a student with a score of at least
    _____ .
    a. 550
    b. 500
    c. 475
    d. 449
    e. 400

21. TOEFL test questions are _____ .
    a. true/false
    b. matching
    c. essay
    d. completion
    e. none of the above

FILLING OUT COLLEGE APPLICATION FORMS

Fill out the following application form. It is for a community college. Then, in small groups, discuss whether the form is similar to others you have filled out. Also, discuss any problems you had in completing it.

PLEASE PRINT CLEARLY

1.

2. LAST NAME   FIRST   MI

3. BIRTHDATE   MONTH - DAY - YEAR

4. AGE

5. [ ] SPRING
[ ] SUMMER   19___
[ ] FALL

APPLICATION FOR

SOCIAL SECURITY NUMBER (Optional)

6. ETHNIC BACKGROUND
(Optional-for research purposes)

1. [ ] Black/Afro American
2. [ ] Chicano/Hispanic Mexican/American
3. [ ] White/Caucasian
4. [ ] Asian/Pacific Islander
5. [ ] American Indian Alaskan Native
6. [ ] Filipino
7. [ ] Other
8. [ ] Decline to State

7. SEX   [ ] MALE   [ ] FEMALE

8. TELEPHONE
Home ( )   Area Code   Number
Bus: ( )   Area Code   Number

9. List other names you have used. If none, check box.   [ ] NONE
Last
First

10. PLACE OF BIRTH
City
State or Foreign Country

11. CITIZENSHIP (Check-One)
1. [ ] US Citizen
2. [ ] Permanent Resident
3. [ ] Foreign Student (F-Visa)
4. [ ] Refugee
5. [ ] Diplomatic (A)
6. [ ] Tourist (B)
7. [ ] Treaty Trader (E)
8. [ ] Temp. Service (H)
9. [ ] Other Visa (Incl. Asylees)

Type of Visa
0. [ ] No Visa
If **NOT** a U.S. Citizen complete the following:

Country of Citizenship
Alien No. or Visa No.
Adjustment Date

12. WHEN DID YOUR PRESENT STAY IN CALIF. BEGIN?
Month   Day   Year

13. LEGAL ADDRESS - DO NOT USE P.O. BOX NO.
Number   Street   Apt. No
City   State   Zip Code
I have lived at this address since   Month   Day   Year
If less than 2 years, list previous address:
No/Street   City/State   Mo/Yr. to Mo/Yr.
No/Street   City/State   Mo/Yr. to Mo/Yr.
Check box if you have a separate Mailing Address

14. HAVE YOU (or if you are under 19, your parents) **EVER**:
YES   NO
Registered to vote in a state other than California?   [ ] [ ]
Petitioned for divorce in a state other than California?   [ ] [ ]
Attended an out of state institution as a resident of that state?   [ ] [ ]
Declared non-residence for California state income tax purposes?   [ ] [ ]

If Yes, What Year

15. COMPLETE THIS SECTION ONLY IF YOU ARE UNDER 19 AND NEVER MARRIED:
Father (if living)   Name
No/Street   City State   Lived in Calif. since
Mother (if living)   Name
No/Street   City State   Lived in Calif. since
Legal Guardian   Name
No/Street   City State   Lived in Calif. since

16. CHECK TYPE OF HIGH SCHOOL CERTIFICATE
Mo.   Yr.
1. [ ] HS Diploma →
2. [ ] GED
3. [ ] Cal. HS Prof. Exam
4. [ ] Cert. of Completion
5. [ ] Foreign Secondary Diploma
6. [ ] Not a high school graduate.
(If currently attending high school what grade will you be in when college classes begin?)   Grade

17. LAST HIGH SCHOOL ATTENDED:
Name of High School
City
State

18. PLEASE CHECK BOX IF
A. You want information on financial aid and assistance.   [ ]
B. You are disabled and want information on special services.   [ ]

19. List ALL colleges or universities previously attended. If none check box   [ ]
Name   City State   Dates Attended   Degree Awarded

20. Number of college semester units/or degree completed as of the beginning of the term for which you are applying.
1 [ ] 0 - 15½
2 [ ] 16 - 29½
3 [ ] 30 - 59½
4 [ ] 60 or more
5 [ ] Associate Degree
6 [ ] BA Degree or Higher

21. Have you previously applied for admission to THIS college:
[ ] Yes   Semester & Year
[ ] No

22. Have you ever enrolled in credit courses at THIS college:
[ ] Yes   Semester & Year
[ ] No
[ ] Community Services Classes Only

23. CERTIFICATION
I declare under penalty of perjury that all information on this form is correct. I understand that falsification or withholding information requested on this form shall constitute grounds for dismissal. I have received a copy of the Student Conduct code.

Signature   Date

NOTICE TO STUDENTS
If additional information is needed to determine your residence status you will be required to complete a supplemental residence question-naire and or to present evidence in accordance with Education Code Sections 68040 et seq. The burden of proof to clearly demonstrate both physical presence in California and intent to establish California residence lies with the student.

OFFICE USE ONLY
Residence Code   Country Code   School Code   Status Code
A O N ___ date

APPLICATION FOR ADMISSION · LOS ANGELES COMMUNITY COLLEGES

CCC

OPEN-ENDED ACTIVITIES

Choose one or more of the following activities to do outside of class. When you finish, tell the class what you've learned.

1. Call or write to request catalogs from your neighborhood community colleges, vocational schools, and university extension programs. Also, get catalogs from the local Y.M.C.A. and parks and recreation departments. Then take some classes of interest to you.

2. Go to your neighborhood college or vocational school and walk around during the semester or quarter. Go to the bookstore, eat in the cafeteria, eavesdrop on the students, and sit in on the large lecture classes, if that's allowed.

3. Write to the TOEFL office and ask for a free bulletin of information and application form:

TOEFL Office
Box 6151
Princeton, NJ 08541